G14/2

G24

POETRY INTRODUCTIONS 1

POETRY INTRODUCTIONS 1

CHRIS ARTHUR
ADRIAN FOX
MATT KIRKHAM
MARIA MCMANUS
FRANCIS O'HARE

LAGAN PRESS
BELFAST
2004

Published by
Lagan Press
Unit 11
1A Bryson Street
Belfast BT5 4ES
e-mail: lagan-press@e-books.org.uk
web: lagan-press.org.uk

ISBN: 1 904652 08 5

Authors: Arthur, Chris; Fox, Adrian;
Kirkham, Matt; McManus, Maria; O'Hare, Francis
Title: Poetry Introductions 1
2004

Set in Sabon
Design: December
Printed by Easyprint, Belfast

Contents

Matt Kirkham

Maria McManus

Francis O'Hare

CHRIS ARTHUR

was born in Belfast in 1955 and lived for
many years in County Antrim. Educated at
Friends' School Lisburn, Campbell College
Belfast and the University of Edinburgh, he
worked as warden on a nature reserve on
the shores of Lough Neagh and as a TV
researcher before moving to Wales in
1989. He currently lectures at the
University of Wales, Lampeter.

He is the author of two collections of
essays, *Irish Nocturnes* (Davies Group,
Colorado, 1999) and *Irish Willow* (Davies
Group, Colorado, 2002). A third volume,
Irish Haiku, is due for publication in 2005.

His poetry has appeared in *The Antigonish
Review*, *The Dalhousie Review*, *Descant*,
The Honest Ulsterman, *Poetry Ireland
Review*, *The Southern Review* and other
journals on both sides of the Atlantic.

Forecasts

I listen to the weather forecasts since our separation,
attentively, as if for news of you,
countries, climate, isobars now add their weight,
giving substance to what seemed unreal at first:
your things packed in the hall,
an engine running in the street outside,
and someone waiting—
like me, in love with you.

The maps and symbols split Europe into two,
where I am, France, a small-town hideaway,
the in-between quite meaningless,
except for all the distance it creates,
then Edinburgh and you.

News bulletins only emphasise the fact,
cruel or kind I am not sure,
that what we really care about
is hard-rooted in the lives of those we love.
If an earthquake ripped through Perpignan,
plague decimated Athens, or more bombs blitzed Belfast,
it would mean less to me than Scottish weather,
picturing the way you pull your collar tight
and hurry in the rain, or smile unfailingly,
delighted by first snow.
Gentle images, but ruthless in their primacy,
easily eclipsing volcanoes, famines, wars.

We stay in touch, sporadic letters, cards,
news of changes of address,
marriages and births and deaths,
brief, polite and formal,
sticking to the rules for strangers,
which we've become again
in our re-invented separateness.

I never guessed when we first met
that there would be a time like this,
when your headlines did not feature me at all.
Perhaps if I had listened better then
to the forecasts of your tears and silences,
I might have spotted storm clouds,
known what rough weather lay ahead.

Codicil

House-calls mean cancer, stroke, first flights,
the realisation that routines will stop,
and that the gentle flow of time,
safe, mundane, meandering,
cannot bear them past death's drought.

After tea and home-made scones
and desultory chat,
I take my notebook out
and we apportion to those left behind,
the house, a favourite piece of jewellery,
some savings, this and that.

Later, I'll draw the parchment up
and come back for a signature.
More tea and pleasantries,
a handshake, then I'm off,
a country lawyer driving on familiar roads,
yet always with a sense of quaysides,
imminent departures, distance,
waving people off.

Sometimes a second thought will bring me back,
a codicil, deletion, double-check,
but usually I don't speak with them again;
after my house-calls I turn necromancer—
speak to the living for the dead.

The matter-of-factness of the act—
'putting their affairs in order'—
is what impresses most.
Behind it no great fear of finitude,
but a horror of untidiness,
consideration for those left to cope.
Biting on the bullet of hard fact,
their no-nonsense eschatology
of courage, resignation, common sense,
conspires to hobble death
more deftly than the theologians like.

Your Gentle Alchemy

Each afternoon, small hands warm the cold keys,
try to unlock the tuneless gravity of silence.
Before them your example: a master-mason's skill,
you play, and weightlessness lifts every note,
cathedrals of pure sound invade the air,
their naves and steeples effortlessly built,
vaults soar and blossom in the ear,
gargoyles cavort,
icebergs of muteness melt at your deft touch
as waterfalls of music come to life.
Coaxed into easy fluency, the native dumbness of the hand,
faltering fingers patiently corrected, straightened, honed,
you distil out of the wort and wash of scales and exercises
the heady miracle of harmony.
The change wrought here makes lead to gold look easy,
just shabby schoolboy conjuring,
your gentle alchemy, no mere Midas touch,
plumbs deeper seams of longing.
If the generals were not mad like most of us,
they'd surround you with a bodyguard of honour—
here at last is something of real worth,
richness beyond the tuneless jewels that we hoard.
The music stops,
jet fighters deafen overhead,
the money markets turn the prayer wheels of desire,
children are starved,
rainforests felled.
Mailed fists smash my keyboard of imagining,
as the ancient tyranny of shoddy values blinks and wakens,
reasserts its old discordant stranglehold upon me.

Provisions

Things you will need,
stowed on the bedside table
for your voyage through the night:
a book, a glass of water, radio,
framed photographs of distant sons,
a torch and telephone, and on a pad
the numbers of the doctor and police.
It is as if I'd found, frail and complete,
the craft of some brave shipwrecked monk,
washed up, dry-beached, light as husk,
a wafer-thin cocoon now hatched and empty
but for these tiny artefacts of faith
in something undefined, impossible,
that might sustain forever
the daily pilgrimage of safe routine.
Bold Brendan's journeys may be done,
but every night old women climb
into their neat suburban coracles
and make heroic voyages,
sail unsung and solitary
across the seas of widowhood.
Their provisions give sparse comfort,
but it is the only comfort that there is.

First Night

This house has always had a voice,
it speaks in creaks and groans as if it was alive.
We got so used to it each night we only noticed
when visitors remarked on it,
or if it woke the children,
made them fearful of some hurt.
'Expansion and contraction',
'Just bricks and timber cooling down'.
'No need to worry'—this was all we said,
our ritual incantations, soothing, rational,
imagined monsters banished by their words,
little stays which shored our courage up,
held our world together through the uninhabitable dark.

A familiar settling of roof beams, floorboards, stairs,
as if each part, tired of a long day's standing with our weight,
shifted its position, sighed, stretched and eased the strain,
re-arranged the burden of our lives,
balancing its cargo in some different way.
In time the sounds became expected, soporific, a lullaby,
we were serenaded into sleep
by the recognized percussive mutters of the house we built.
For years we spilled our dreams and laughter into it,
poured out our youth around its well-worn shapes,
time's wax into its mould, lovemaking, nakedness, cupped safe
behind these eggshell walls and curtained windows,
our lives held in this niche by all the gentle tyrannies of place.

Now you are not here the sounds have changed,
as if your presence, sitting in the chair, was some
    familiar mountainside,
a known landmark, at which the house, like some gigantic bat,
aimed its vocabulary of radar, a tongue of creaks
    and groans and taps,
and got a stream of echoes back, spelling out safe bearings,
our intimate landscapes minutely mapped.

Now what was friendly, dull, benign,
tonight seems eerie, almost terrifying.
The house sounds lost, a banshee flying blind,
looking for the braille of small routines and known directions:
your key turned in the lock, your tread upon the stairs,
nudging its familiar territory of known time and space
   with sound,
but finding only unfamiliar absence there.
The house and I cry desperately together,
probe ahead with tearful sonar,
try to steer some course through loss's dreadful weather.
(I know this must sound fanciful,
but it is the best way I can think of to describe
my first night here alone for forty years.)

Remembering our first night here together, the house just built,
the smell of new-sawn timber, fresh mortar, paint still wet,
and us two together in one bed at last,
our bodies' joists learning to take new weights,
dovetailing snugly into each other's waiting space,
settling into sounds and movements, echoed by the house itself,
that spelt out who we were for four decades.
After the funeral, sitting here alone,
it seemed as though some part of me had been cut off,
as if a room, or everything upstairs, had been sheared away,
but knowing it so well I still pace round its confines,
the echoes of my footsteps sound unreal and it is hard to tell
this awful present moment from my memories,
establish what is lost and what still here.

Companionless, I reach back into time for moorings,
   for some sounding board,
find my mother waiting there and hers before her, going
   back in line;
each one married, mated, widowed, left alone again,
re-learning in old age familiar places made alien by absence,
places where they'd lain once in sleep, in love, in childbirth,
their first nights with houses, husbands, children, corpses.

I picture my beginnings amidst the clean raw smell
    of bricks and timber,
and mingled in, the scent of damp caves, skins, flint, woodsmoke,
a whiff of ghostly sisterhood in loss, the fragility of habitation,
our tiny houses, caves and huts like limpets on the rock
    of time itself,
the ring-fence of the human family, strangers made
    almost intimate.

And I wonder if the world sounds different every night
    as people come and go,
my ear attuned too long to smaller scales has lost its range,
and I am deaf to all the bigger notes: God, destiny,
the meaning of it all, life after death.
My horizons have been drawn in
to husband, children, house, health, garden, shops,
but tonight it sounds as if the rafters of the planet
creak and groan and try to speak.
My landmarks send no homely echoes back,
as if I were a child again, I imagine monsters in the dark,
formless, terrible,
but there is no one here to say 'No need to worry', 'All is well',
chant soothing incantations to dispel my fear,
I recite them to myself, but somehow that is not the same.
Suddenly the reassurance of the past,
the massive mute companionship of bleak inevitability,
hard though it is, is the only straw of comfort I can grasp.

Swifts

The swift is one of the most remarkable birds. It spends most of its time on the wing, non-breeding birds even roosting in flight; it mates in the air after wild flights in which parties of screaming birds take part. It takes all its insect food in flight, and collects its nesting material of airborne feathers, grass stems and other plant fragments without landing.

—Oxford Book of Birds

As lions sculpt the gracefulness of antelope,
so swifts, like wild dogs of the air, quarter the sky,
and by their deft transactions keep it sheer and stark,
pluck from the eye of space feathers, twigs and particles,
flotsam of sluggish cloud and lazy blue,
snatched on the wing and hoarded in the dark.

Have the sharp scythe-shapes of swifts,
like shrapnel from some distant blast,
ever cut across a serpent's eye,
igniting in some dry sulcus of the brain
a blaze of secret swift dreams, airy fantasies?
To shrug off for a while the heavy coils of gravity
and dream snake-dreams of soaring on high,
of unimpeded distance, seeding space itself with life,
grazing on the very stratosphere, hatching out
   a clutch of eggs
high in the rafters of a wind-borne nest,
seeing the sky as now they see the earth ...

To die, I picture them ascending ever faster,
further and yet further to tremendous height,
then folded close, clenched tight into themselves,
dropping like a feathered meteorite.
Their tiny bow unstrung at last,
the wings which shot a thousand flights compacted
   to an arrowhead,
it hits the ground so fast the corpse fragments,
erupts into a thousand shards of swift,

and from its ground-burst heart, bright as a gem,
which powered this splinter-ship across the world,
some dark and secret iris roots and flowers,
to scent the sky with haunting odours, fleet and sharp;
the tribe of swifts above keen and rejoice,
as if their flight was choreographed
by perfume only they can grasp.

In Marchmont Cemetery, Edinburgh

Brains filled with thoughts of Jesus lie rotted row by row,
cornflakes, cat food, bread and milk, he died to save us
    from our sins,
coffee, tea bags, prayers, eternity and cigarettes;
new shoes, rent a video, Christ our saviour,
    dentist ten o'clock—
the muddled familiarity of shopping lists, decay,
    salvation, death,
held in the tunnels of the mind for years.
Now they've collapsed,
pit-props of daily purpose sagged and snapped,
the cargo of their talk has all spilled out,
and all that's left is silent,
entombed beneath the well-kept grass.

Tongues that loaded words for years into the sea of emptiness,
reclaiming from it some dry land of seeming sense,
with talk of promised lands, long life, good health,
lie cold and still, drowned by the slow waves of the earth,
the pious dust of churchgoers mixed in with sinners' dirt,
both lend the millimetric weight and substance of their dust
to bolster the firm upthrust of ground against my living tread.

And blooming round the headstones, dandelions,
and in a new-leafed tree a watchful blackbird on its nest,
and schoolgirls just outside the gate,
and all the while
the thrust of sap against the bark,
sky-blue eggs cupped warm in mud,
the yellow pigment of worm-hungry beaks,
the smooth skin of a virgin's thigh untouched as yet.

Shorn of its trumpets, day of judgement, wrath,
the elements of fearful faith,
as one thing unravels slowly into something else
resurrection is made ordinary,
miraculous.

Appearances Can Be Deceptive
Four random extracts from a continuing series of observations

I
Standing Back
    'You have to stand back from things,'
    so they tell me, 'see them in the right perspective'.
    Sometimes it feels that I've been walking backwards
        all my life
    to try to see things as they should be seen.
    The world seems permanently out of focus,
    a slapstick, sct-up photograph, farcical and obvious:
    step by step reversing towards the drop,
    unfathomable and ever present at my back.

II
Vacuum Cleaner
    A plug-in python, comatose for days.
    Digestion, like recurrent death, imposes silence, immobility,
    before each foray from its cupboard lair
    to snake through carpet undergrowth
    and draw in dirt and dust again.
    A noisy boa, sucking to constrict,
    its prey, stale household plankton,
    ever plentiful.
    Once engorged it slinks home,
    belly full and holds its breath.

III
Morality
    They told me later, when I was being charged,
    that throwing paint at someone else's property,
    stand-in blood, a warning of impending massacre,
    was childish, an over-reaction to the fact
    that missiles that could end the world tonight
    are stacked in silos round my home.
    So I asked them, if that's what you believe,

why don't you walk on your hands,
speak backwards,
feel hungry when you eat?
And I have a sudden vivid picture in my mind
(criminal, deranged, of course)
of upside-down policemen, politicians,
judges, worthy citizens,
all disapproving of my crazy uprightness.
Then I remember that the mechanism of the eye
involves interpreting inversion all the time.
Perhaps that's what morality's become,
so instant a realigning of the upside-down
that what is mad seems sane,
and what is right seems wrong.

IV
Theologian
Sometimes in TV reports of ultramodern sewage works,
we see pictures of enormous vats of waste,
slow moving, foul, great stagnant pools of filth.
Then, almost miraculous,
via abstruse filters, after miles of taps and tubes,
a glass of reclaimed water, clear and pure, is ready
    to be drunk;
the visiting celebrity smiles to camera, downs it in a gulp.
The theologian tries to work like this,
distilling all our anguish into something we can use.
No alchemist pursued a wilder dream than this:
no short leap of faith from lead to gold,
no mere water into wine,
but heaven sluiced through every crumb of earth.
Yet each time that I try to drink down what he says,
I gag on every mouthful.
In each sip, unmistakable,
the taste of raw blood,
excrement
and death.

Beyond Aughlish

'In the name of God, Amen. I, John Arthur, of Aughlish in the County of Londonderry, being weak in body but of sound mind, memory and judgement, do make this my last will and testament in manner following. First, I leave and bequeath my soul to God who gave it ... '
—from my great-grandfather's will, dated 24th January, 1884

I

Among our campfire-catch of maxims, mottoes,
    superstitions, spells—
shoals of folk-wisdom netted in a trice of words,
and brought up now and then to punctuate some current
    incident with 'this is how it is', 'the world is thus',
the bittersweet of raw experience trawled by a hundred
    generations and honed to shapes familiar to the touch,
a fixed belief, confirmed by those who, unexpectedly,
    have lived,
that somehow, just before you die, your life jumps
    clear of all forgetfulness,
and, like a leaping salmon, flashes past, shocking
    in its sudden wholeness and unexpected nakedness.

II

Perhaps there is some truth in this, or maybe wishful
    thinking is at work,
or habit merely reaching for the nearest tools to hand,
    their handles shiny with accustomed use.
I do not know the ins and outs of it, great-grandfather,
only, as I read your will, imagined dying, attended
    at my father's death,
something flashed out from the depths which seemed
    to fill this old, familiar, comfortable net,
until I tried to pull it in: 'Before you die your whole life
    flashes past'—
the net broke open, the gaff flew wildly from my grip.

III

Beyond Aughlish the spotlight fades, the faces
  of the troupe grow dim,
blend mutely, indistinct as stone, into the backdrop
  of small County Londonderry fields and farms.
Your will, handwritten, browned with age, digs down
  into the words till water comes,
a small ditch in the waterlogged expanse of time
  which irrigates, allows the sodden anonymity of history
  to drain and flow.
I wade into our past, feel names and dates and places
  cohere into flesh and blood again.
My line of tumblers, lion tamers, fools, trace out a vein
  of vanished venues and performances,
umbilical, to where the big top first was raised.

IV

Aughlish, our names, all that we say, a chain of words
  passed on from hand to hand,
hearthstones of semi-sense to shield us from the sun
  in whose heat we perform our lives away,
a drystone wall across the undivided, untamed
  countryside,
behind which we have juggled, farmed and fed
  and warred and multiplied,
a big top, canvas taut against the wind, inside a sea
  of sawdust littered with the flotsam of each act
  like afterbirth—
reach down, find axe-heads, mirrors, rusted bicycles,
  cave paintings, faded photographs.

V

I suckle through a single thread the flavour of a costume
  rich beyond the mesh of taste,
guddle with a cobweb touch a catch which outweighs

every breaking strength,
bait my own line with seed sown far beyond
    my tidal depths,
from your trapeze to mine, a swing, a drop, flesh clasped
    to flesh, a salmon leap,
neat images which seemed to order, irrigate, collide
    and blur,
this is how it is, the world is thus, each hook slips
    off the perfect smoothness of the way things are,
we are reduced to desperate epitaphs, tight sayings,
    ringside formula:

VI

In the name of God, Amen, Sometimes your whole life
    flashes past, Do you take this woman, Dust to dust ...
we grasp at straws, our tackle shines with use
    and ignorance,
I wield it clumsy in my hands, hack a rough clearing
    for my act,
knowing that beyond Aughlish and all our other
    wordy craft,
the dark world dwarfs and crowds our little circus tent,
    partners every act with mute impenetrableness
blows our sawdust platforms to the wind and throws us
    into orbits which outleap every will and testament.

Magpies

One for sorrow, two for joy, three for a girl,
four for a boy, five for silver, six for gold,
seven for a secret never to be told.

— Traditional rhyme

It's easy to expand our range:
  Eight for envy, nine for gain,
  ten for an old man left out in the rain ...
But such little steps of ordinary progression can't contain
the burgeoning brutality of numbers;
we would need epic poems to keep pace.
Multiplied beyond the childish abacus of memory—
the spiralling galaxies,
cells in our bodies,
earth's population,
time's duration,
the distance between stars—
the magpies swarm like flies,
mock the paltry reach of rhyme,
their numbers rob words' nests of meaning,
evade every stratagem of neat confinement.

We watch helpless as they strut and peck their way
through all of language's attempted cages,
release a gaudy raucousness out of the mundane.
Last night fifty chattered on the eaves of speech,
like vultures, waiting for the death of certainty,
today a thousand mobbed us as we talked,
the air around us clogged,
soft gagging feathers in the throat,
tomorrow sees a million massing on the tongue,
their secret never to be told made common knowledge:
beneath each flimsy labelling name and number
    (always, constant),
anonymous, uncounted, the brute unrhyming fact,
our raw, incredible existence.

31

Departures

The drama of our obvious departures—
airports, stations, docks—
scenes of ritualised leave-taking,
anticipated, practised,
their goodbyes scripted out—
obscures the fact that
every moment of our lives we bid farewell
to some small part of our brief stake in time,
and that some unknown moment of an ordinary day,
mundane and unannounced,
will be the last we spend on Earth,
some casual sentences spoken to a friend
will utterly conclude the sum of what we said.

The weight of imminent departure,
time's gravity,
is the pressure we are hatched to,
so constant as it leans its weight upon us
it does not seem real.
Yet if it somehow ceased to be,
and eternity opened out before us,
our lives, like deep-sea fishes
lifted from the dark unnoticed tonnage of their depths,
would disintegrate, explode,
for we are creatures of departure;
it is the air we breathe,
the unseen water that surrounds us.

Climbing

Time cupped its hands for eighty years
to take the pressure of his voice,
and then let go—
sent spinning into silence
the soft tread of each utterance,
and we who knew the inclines of those notes so well,
watched helpless as we saw them tumbling to extinction.
We talked about our sadness and the sense of loss:
'It's better that he went and did not suffer more',
reconciled by specious logic to the hard fact
    of life's gravity,
knowing everyone will fall.

We rearrange our tackle and go on.
A piton less, a rope frayed through, a harness torn,
another contour of our map rubbed out,
we close ranks and revise our route,
our ear tunes in to other footholds,
and voices that will never sound again
fade from memory's vertigo,
then are gone for good.

And sometime, time,
which used to measure out familiar climbs—
from breakfast until lunch,
from nine till five,
from when you waved goodbye
till when we held each other close again—
will one day measure out
the last five words we ever speak,
unclench all its fingers,
spill our various ascents.

Nostos

The greatest shock is finding we're still here,
as if this place ignored the fact of absence,
like a trifling insult forgotten between friends,
and stubbornly retained our image on its streets,
holding cupped in unexpected hands
a hundred prison chalices of memory,
and when I drink, the flavours of the past are all released.
A plain and patient lover enduring separation stoically,
our photographs well dusted on some inner mantelshelf,
it is as if this undistinguished suburb,
with no claim to note beyond familiarity,
was waiting, faithful as a gin trap, for return.
Now I am the warmth whose passing
makes the writing of our lives appear again—
for years our history was inscribed
upon the little contours of this place,
the story of our childhood indelible,
in time's strange disappearing ink.
For all the change that's happened here:
new houses built, trees felled, new roads,
strangers in the house we used to live in;
a sense of knowing still remains, durable as blood.
I can lay no claim to ownership of course,
time shrugs off each tenant's poor attempt
    at permanence,
but passing through I feel, co-mingled and confused,
a sense of alienation and companionship.
And yet young mothers with their children
    watch suspiciously;
I am not known here, evicted by the years
and turned into a dangerous loiterer where I once played,
as safe and innocent of what was yet to come
as their children running now across our lawn.
I pass the places where we used to be and see us there,
not knowing anything of who we'd come to be,
and think of then and now, and us strung out between them,

living ligatures upon the rack of years,
and wonder (who has not?) if I could reach back,
trim my sails, set the tiller on a different course,
who I would be now, freed from these chains
    of circumstance
and bound in others.
Whatever destiny we have, real or daydreamed,
when we are gone beyond return,
is there some way to access history again,
superheat the page of yesterday with some
    incandescent flame?
Being here today makes me almost feel the heat
    upon my face,
awakening from the pages of this place,
yellowed with age, all time's silenced syllables,
and as they wake all thoughts of home disintegrate;
algae, amoebas, dinosaurs, dogs, apes,
our shadowy progenitors, fracture the familiar,
draw from its customary sheath
the strangeness that, unnoticed, attends
    the most mundane,
and let it cut to ribbons all thought of the quotidian.

Wildebeest Theology

'There is no room within the Christian thought-world for the idea of tragedy in any sense that includes the idea of finally wasted suffering.'
—John Hick, *Evil and the God of Love*

'Of the 39 kills we have timed, all but one took no more than 5 minutes before death occurred. In the one remaining instance, a yearling wildebeest caught by a pack of four wild dogs took 17 minutes to die.'
—Hugo van Lawick, *Innocent Killers*

Stands oblivious as abstract seconds tick away,
pegged like a tent caught by four gin trap jaws,
caught up upon the ratchet whir of concrete time,
pain consumes its dying consciousness.

The canvas of the hide is ripped and torn,
and pain, corkscrewed into many teeth and claws,
bores down the guy-line thread of nerve,
then barbed and hooked, tugs and withdraws.

Slow or fast of small importance here,
speed can command no succour when time is thrown
    out of gear,
and pain drills its own dark regiments of seconds,
relentless, into months and years.

Theodicy takes every episode of anguish,
exonerates God's love despite appearance,
and, with a stopwatch out of step with living,
times some distant purpose, all good and all forgiving.

Throughout its dusty pages all I hear
is expert savagery, the slow tick-tock of pain,
Auschwitz, cancer, death by slow degrees,
the dog pack's frenzied noises.

Ghost Dance

*A Chinese fingerprint expert has discovered what he believes
to be the world's oldest fingerprint, left seven thousand years
ago by a potter on a water jar.*

Cheyenne, Arapaho, Apache, Sioux—
the words themselves strong medicine,
talismans that magic into view a mix of images:
wigwams, warpaint, moccasins,
magnets that pull into the hold of memory
TV detritus littering the mind's seabed.
Buoyant at the mention of the names,
woodcraft, harmony with nature,
cruelty, rise up from there,
awesome endurance of inflicted pain,
firewater, arrows, braves and squaws,
sheer tough competence with living.

And yet for all their skill and iron,
more deadly than their deadliest war-party,
more silent than their silentest of stalkers,
more fearless than the bravest of their warriors,
there is another tribe that dwarfs them.

Its braves have passed in droves across our doors,
they weave in and out of everywhere we go,
their infiltration is complete.
We are surrounded and outnumbered.
We cannot keep them out,
but for the most part we ignore them,
or pretend they are not there,
or look away,
suppose the wagons of the everyday
drawn into circles of routine like musk oxen,
can see off any threat of change.

We remember we are shadowed, stalked and hunted
only when we hear a twig that snaps behind us,
accidentally stumble on some faint betraying traces,
churchyards, castles, history books, old photographs,
a fingerprint, dreams of dead remembered faces.
Smoke signals drifting through the years,
that tell of kinship, loss and longing,
totems of the splintered human nation.

Seven thousand years away my new blood-brother beckons,
proffers the water jar he's firing,
like a lazy tomahawk thrown across the centuries
to cleave a line between the dead and living,
time's chalice offered to his new-found sibling.
One day I know I'll join him, change tribes
and leave behind as little trace as he has—
papooses fathered, houses built, a few tasks done,
the stuff of our impermanence like the whorls of tiny lines,
the cobwebs of our touch, feeling's fragile contour maps,
that sink back into flatlands where there once were alps,
as we shuffle towards the past in our perpetual ghost dance.

Atiq

'When an Inuit baby is a few days old it is given its atiq. *This* atiq, *usually translated as name, constitutes its essence or soul. This 'soul', however, is someone else. Among most Inuit, the newborn's* atiq *is an old relative who has died, frequently a grandparent or great-uncle or aunt. For the rest of its life, those who do not know the child will ask:* 'kinamik atirqarpit?', *'whom do you have as an* atiq?".

—Hugh Brody, *Living Arctic*

We are ourselves alone, walking on air,
'I' is the ousting cuckoo in the nest,
breath drawn from the shallow well of self,
its memory stops a stone's-throw from the here and now,
history-less, the long umbilical of kinship severed,
the gravity of ancestry ignored, the present swelled,
perspective in our world is unreal as a dream:
we live as though the past does not concern us.

The stale warm air of wards and day rooms,
illness, frailty, the smell of musty attics, death,
confines to nursing homes and trunks and funerals
the spirit of those gone before.
Forgotten names and faded photographs clot
    our bloodlines,
crust with the crude assumptions of neglect
the depths of time, make slight its wealth.

We move across a surface that we make,
the glittering meniscus of forgetfulness,
pond-skaters gliding on our planes of ignorance,
we have slipped our moorings from the fleet
and imagine that we sail alone,
take our position from the dull stars that we make:
career, possessions, travel, news and sex,
called after film stars, footballers, long-forgotten saints.

39

But surviving in the blood and breath,
immune to every mutiny,
our heavy cargo undeclared:
'Kinamik atirqarpit?'
raises from the seeming dead
a lost Atlantis;
the smuggled world
there below the waterline of self.

Antecedents

Caught fleetingly upon this unknown frame of person,
your face, strange in its body's garb of mourning,
looking sad with exactly your expression,
a hundred years ago.
These yellowed pictures,
like messages in bottles,
leave haunting signs,
sun-worn, sea-faded,
tell of something lithe and ancient,
marooned on distant living islands
yet drawing closer every second.

From quiver in the mud to hominid,
across an archipelago of lives,
it dances out, hopscotch, escaping,
on each stepping stone, the map of history.
I see you in your great-grandmother as widow,
the farmer's bride, young, full of buxom promise,
the distant cousin whose name you can't remember,
your mother as a pretty schoolgirl,
and before them all, unnamed but still familiar,
animating other features, part of someone else's drama,
I can picture further antecedents.

The photographs, like footprints,
far more than just some family's cache of memories,
are a fragment of itinerary,
of something carried down bloodlines,
formed and reformed a billion times,
in you, your ancestors, our children's children,
an awesome journey, at once hallowing and dwarfing;
a sense of links and chains and relays,
passing on from sea to land, from cold to warmth,
from death to life, from hand to hand,
the fire of something living.

Looking at the photographs brought back to mind
old stories of a single creature sundered into two,
who, shunning its unnatural separateness,
spends eternity searching for its twin.
I scan the faces of the men posed stern beside you,
looking for my own reflection there,
anonymous, among these unknown fellow seekers,
led helpless by your grail,
possessed and yet unreachable.

And as I stare,
I feel scar tissue running from my head to foot,
a tribal mark, the sign of mute blood-brotherhood,
only in embrace with you is it unzipped and healed.
The scar, umbilical, erotic,
promising reunion, separation, longing,
the searing whiplash nerve of feeling,
coils its way through human being,
blurring our ending and beginning.

Satori Splinters

*'Haiku are a kind of satori, or enlightenment,
in which we see into the life of things.'*

—R.H. Blyth

Your last words on earth
mix with strident TV sounds,
here in this bleak ward.

Midway through my list,
baked beans, bread, potato crisps,
I remember death.

Look at the reptiles!
Curios in glass prisons—
once they ruled the world.

The ghosts of insects,
snowflakes numerous as flies.
Unbuzzing winter.

Miles from anywhere
only one light cracks the dark.
Moths tap-tap the pane.

A city season:
cherry blossom on the road
made snow by headlights.

'All life is sacred.'
Old school mottoes once believed—
people die like flies.

We were strangers once.
Intimacy, accident—
the years soon vanish.

ADRIAN FOX

was born in Kent, England. His family moved to Belfast in 1967. He studied creative writing under the tutelege of the late Ulster poet James Simmons.

His work has been widely published in various magazines including *Cyphers*, the *Honest Ulsterman*, *Poetry Ireland Review*, *Black Mountain Review*, *Poetry Society* and *Coffee House*. A selection of his work appeared in the recent anthology *Breaking the Skin* (Black Mountain Press, 2002). A pamphlet *Hide Dada, Hide* appeared from Lapwing Press in 1999.

A songwriter as well as poet, he teaches creative writing in the Armagh area and currently works as the Verbal Arts Officer at the Millennium Court Arts Centre in Portadown.

The Light on the Stones

I retrace your final journey now in a blue car,
not black, alone on the motorway.
Passing the Maze prison, the stench of my engine
overheating is like gunpowder, spent shells,
lingering, your dream of Irish freedom.

I climbed the mountain graveyard
above the violent divided city,
above the peace line that stood between us
in the living room. It was a maze
of kept graves, lawns, wreaths, flowers,
names on glistening headstones.

Your plot all weeds,
and wild grass cries out for order.
The fallen wooden cross bears no name;
but you are there. Like a sculptor
with clay I reach inward, my hands
as delicate as salmon wings riding
the white water, struggling
the strong currents of grief.

I brush the soiled tears from your eyes
and you wake in me, swimming
and glistening in mine. My hands
shape the clay moulding our wounded past,
emerging in the light on the stones.

Wait for me to lie down on the grass, on the weeds
on the boulder you rest your head upon.

My Father's Bedroom

A single bed and someone's
discarded wardrobe.
One suit hanging like
your life, your death.

The thick scent of your grease
and body odour I recall
familiar from my childhood.

The grime of your toil lingering
there on the pillow and soiled
bedclothes of your dreams.

They scurried through the house
raising carpets and floorboards,
certain of treasures to claim.

I went to the window and lifted
the blemished, fragile curtain,
my breath fell with yours, stale

on the cold transparency.
I left with nothing, apart from
that thick scent I thought

was lost until today.

Saint Luke's
for Stephanie

Ward 6, Cell 8, is my address here.
What is this place I volunteered for,
winding corridors like the confusion of my mind
that lead to anxiety, suicidal tendencies,
the elderly and the deranged?
Hopefully they will lead back to me,
my children out there in the world wandering
avenues and streets the same colour as my cell.

I remember when I used to laugh at people
who were off-centre, saying they were ready
for St. Luke's, and here I am, knocked off.
The old stumble past, stooping closer
to the soil with each shuffling step,
mumbling for the price of a cup of tea
or a cigarette I can't afford to oblige.

The shakes have dwindled to a pulse
and the sweating flushes have subsided.
I looked at myself in the mirror today
and noticed that the wild snake veins
no longer disturb the whites of my eyes.
I got a card from my Daughter, it said,
'I'm proud of you Mum, for trying.'

Half a Sestina for Stephanie

How can I write a sestina for you:
six stanzas of six lines concluding death,
killing yourself in a three-line envoy?
I, who doesn't know the time of day
when the lines of your life were diverted
to lie low in the blue-stoned soil?

Reliving grief, my hands delve in the soil
moulding a clay figurine of you.
Retracing the black paths that diverts
my gaze away from the sunset to death.
A photograph of you on your wedding day
your smile didn't convey love's envoy.

Was it back then that the messenger
whispered phlegmed words that soiled
your soul to fall early to your funeral day?
Did a touch reach out and abuse you
fondling filthy caresses to die
out there on the back roads where diverted

diversions took you
round and round
to fall foul of the dead end?

Unapproved Roads
for Jimmy Simmons

I'm approaching this poem as you would—
head on. We drove from Craigavon to Letterkenny
hospital, just the two of us in Tom's people-carrier
past the motorway's fresh graffiti: UVF CHILD KILLERS.
Across the Ballygawley roundabout Tom lost track
of where he was going and why, circling twice.

The issue diverted to a run-down unoccupied farm
and the dream of restoration. I tried to sleep
as the night before was one of those nights
when my head was a sieve for the debris of years.
You woke me in the front lobe of my brain,
reciting 'Night Song from a Previous Life'.

I wanted to go off down some unapproved road
but you held me and I found you in a ward slumped
in the chair at the side of a bed. You wanted to pull
the tube that feeds you from your wisdom through
your throat and out your nose, to tear the tracheotomy
out and let your aneurysm bleed free on the floor.

I sit here at my desk during one of your golden moments,
the birds in the dawn rise behind me and I look up,
red wine at my elbow, a pint of stout and your inspiration.
I want to go there myself and do it for you, to let you
roam free on unapproved roads, picking through
the berries of memory to find the ripened cluster.

Stained Glass
i.m. Jimmy Simmons

The summer sun ricocheted
off a Bloody Foreland, freeing
a winter's cold rock face.

Held like the mirrored words
of your poems, skimming
the water with undulated joy.

Creating ripples on the surface
that streamed through the plain
windows of Killalt Church.

Staining them with the colours
of poetry, music and song.

Cold Turkey
lament for a friend

The sharp white water stabs the shore of Lough Neagh
like the harsh tides that engulfed your young life.
The rain, hail, sleet and snow cut the sky
and the congregation's exposed skin.
It was as if the heavens opened to let you in
and the world cried for you, the one without faith.

It all seemed so right, beautiful,
in the ruins of Ardboe Abbey.
I watched your mother's tears, your coffin
circling the Celtic cross three times like
the ritual of motherhood, as if the cold
stone was sculpted by your hands.

As I watched you fall into the earth
I remembered your eyes—
darkened depths as if death itself was your gaze.
You the judge and jury sentenced in a hallucinogenic trial.
You never looked over your shoulder, that powdered look
never high on air. Now that temporary nirvana is gone
and you are finally, permanently stoned,
below a Celtic cross by the shores of the Lough
beneath the sacred earth of Ardboe Abbey.

We stand here above you praying, crying, waiting
for the prayer to end, shivering, dripping wet.

Undyed

The notion of some infinitely gentle,
infinitely suffering thing —T.S. Eliot

My time seemed to stop still, sitting
embracing this complete sentence.
Waiting for my pen to bleed and congeal.

Any minute now, something will happen.
Suddenly I'm distracted, softly teasing
shag tobacco from its pouch like
a weaver spinning thread.

My rough thick hands folding it delicately
into the fine fragile paper with the precision
of placing my sleeping child in bed
without waking.

I wish this poem could capture the shadow
of smoke upon this page, flowing
infinitely gentle in its suffering.

I flicked open Ted Hughes' *Birthday Letters*
at 'Afterbirth' and my wife came in and stood
with a look of defeat, it didn't take, she said
they're still pink.

The film of rain on this November day
trickling on the pane. The trees bare
and ruthless, daggers thrust into the sky.

The offal roots of amniotic dreams, tangled
soul food slithering from a stainless bowl,
nursed into a yellow plastic bag.

Crushed velvet curtains draped undyed
on the kitchen floor seeping evening skies.

Ray River

Although I'm here in Donegal and not Yakima,
Washington state, or in Dublin reclining
on the banks of the Grand Canal,
I feel a sense that Raymond Carver
and Patrick Kavanagh are here with me
following the Ray River to the sea
of this poem.
The winds sway the reeds reflecting
on the rippling water, on a bend a stream
flows into the Ray, cascading on the rocks.
I love the music of this place, the silent
harmonies of the source, the spring,

Falling from high on Muckish mountain
to where I sit translating nature to poetry.
Further on another stream flows in ever
so quiet, secretly subtle, like the clarity
of wonder in the undercurrents.
I'm here at the sea, the reservoir.
Tory Island looms black, remote above
the wild white waves, poetry echoing
across the golden strand.
The colours of a rainbow rise from the sea,
the intangible essence that lingers here.
The blending colours fade to blue
and I feel a slight tingle on my fingers.
I look down to see a multicoloured spider
crawling across my hand and the open
pages of this notebook, as if that
were its only purpose.

Nucella

for Robert Lowell
Imperfection is the language of art—Robert Lowell

I was reading your biography by Ian Hamilton;
during the 15th chapter I discarded the bookmark,
a postcard I bought in Galway.
The title was: Happy Dogwelk (Nucella).
Your finger the pale shade of marine life
blending with starfish and seaweed, pointing
to the seabed.

Now I know where I stand in your intricate
hard waters.

I sit here at the dining-room table, filled
with whiskey, beer and poetry.
I look up into a mirror that shows my way
upstairs, if I dare move from this spot
and chance my way into the reflection
of the first day of March.
Then, only then, will I descend the stairwell
of my youth.

'Dolphin'—
'My eyes have seen what my hand did.'

I wish I had known you,
even to say hello in the street.
To know why I cry on your words,
to know why I cry, Full Stop.

'cire perdue'
for John Behan

The clouds of an overcast sky
Hang over us at the foot of Croagh Patrick,
Eroding the flesh of our blighted past.

Freed as if by a bare-footed pilgrim,
A lost wax process revealing bones
Melting in the tear ducts of our eyes.
Indentations scarred by the artist's hand
Niggling the shadows of sensation.
Emotional turmoil in the skeletal flow.

Skulls open to the wind and rain rest
Hard on pelvic bronze, metacarpals
Insert phalanges in a vertebrae mast.
Parietal bones that hold the hull of Eire.

Blue

The harbour wall holds the fishermen
in a stone grasp, embracing the shore
like naked lovers embedded in the sand.
The swishing swirl of casting lines
weeps like poetry in the air.
A reel screeches, blue pain of the ocean.
Hands grip the rod, the tourniquet.

The captured solitary one struggles,
dragged from the bed of aquamarine.
The crack of flesh on concrete,
sapping the earth, the sea.
The last flickering colour grey, steel,
hate, prize, the swishing swirl
of casting lines shivers blue.

Clare Glen

The car park was empty, but
for the sound of the river
rushing under the bridge.

We could have put
the front passenger seat back
or we could have been
one on the back seat.

Dusk was falling,
red and blue emerging
almost black.

My hand in yours
the sound of the river
was all we had to go on
as the path began to disappear.

All that was left of the day
was a clump of bluebells
shining from the thicket of trees.

We walked on until
we could not find our way,
our clothes strewn among the debris
and moss on the bed of forest.

The rain fell through the canopy
caressing the leaves, branches,
falling on my lips, in your ear,
on your clit, my tongue.

Our bodies illuminating
the forest floor like leaf mould,
lichen sparkling in the night.

Before Dawn

Bathed in artificial light
reading Eamonn Grennan's
'Still Life with Waterfall'.

The harsh tick of the kitchen clock
beats every syllable, grasping
the stinging absence of a wedding ring
thrown from a bedroom window.

The sudden noise of a flock of magpies,
too many for any silly superstitious verse
feasting on yesterday's leftovers.

Nervously, the black feathers blue
looking in on, a single solitary robin
redbreast devours what's left on the plate.

The alarm goes off upstairs
and the top half of the house
shifts out of sleep, swaying;

the birds are gone, the plate is empty,
so I switch off the light.

Traditional Back Roads
for Paddy & Tim

Every time I close my eyes
all I see is the road. Round
and round a ring a ring of Kerry,
like lines drawn on scraps of paper.

A child's version of a tourist map
with scribbles stating YOU ARE HERE!
Arrows that point the way to Inch,
Castleisland, Fieries, Farranfore,
Cille Airne across the Annagh Bog.

Along Paddy Jones' tablature bow marks
to shoot the arrows along the Glen-
aruddery mountain roads with the speed
of a jig, reel, polka or the potholed
puncture in the Black Water drawing
out like a slow air.

Remembering landmarks scarring
the Kerry landscape like the story
of a tragic life, the statue of Padraic
O'Keefe makes me turn left to find
his picture on an old album sleeve.

The tracks of his face as worn
as the bow and fiddle, ingrained
with the stench of porter and whiskey
plucked from the wall of the bar.

I've escaped those traditional back roads,
shot free from on the line accompanied
by Tim O'Shea, lost like, 'The rhythm before
it becomes a beat'. A mark in a music book
diddly-deeing it all the way through Limerick,
Nenagh, Athlone, Cavan, Monaghan
and on home to close my eyes.

The Gap

An aquamarine light spills through the window
and drowns me. Muckish, I must have dreamt.
I woke and you were untranslatable, a strange light
came from behind you as if William Blake had
something to do with it. The way your subtle
dawn touch can paint the contours creating
a landscape not even hinted at in the light of day.
God could be involved here but I hope it's just
another beautiful accident. I watch a crow swoop
down and land on a sheep's back and peck
nesting material from her and fly off into
the trees—only the young lamb thinks this odd,
startled by nature's strange behaviour.
A car flies round the corner and disappears
into the gap of insignificance—man hasn't got
much to do with this landscape and this land-
scape hasn't got much to do with man. Where
would that bird sit if the wire wasn't there?

Splinter
for Eamon Grennan

'I'll never carry another coffin with you,'
you said as we shook hands and you departed.

Before that I never knew you from Adam.
I had to ask someone to point you out,

to stand tall as a pallbearer stands.
Since then I have read your poems.

The remnant of a fibre brushed off
by a flaw on the backbone of the coffin.

That line sticks in my head like a splinter
from a shroud of linen these words can't tweezer out.

Rockpools

The buzz of the tent's zip opens the day
a skylark, the toss of the sea.
I move down from the hills of Connemara,
down with the shifting light.

My shadow on the shore of Renvyle
like an island, the ocean reveals to me
a stone thrown up from the bile of the sea.
I move down through the black rock
veined in white marble.

I look down to see her formed in stone
among the rockpools, her breast swells
the ocean left behind one weeps into a pool.
I move further into the deep ravine

Where the sound of children on the beach
falls silent. I'm alone with her, the elegant
contours of her flesh formed by the sea.
Her torso falls away beneath the pool
of salted water, her bodily fluids

seep from the pink encrustations
of her womb to the broken shells.
Her head is enormous, holding
the secrets she cries white-marbled tears.
She knows violence and speaks

with a barnacled tongue, she's like some
thing created by Picasso or Henry Moore.
She's my Connemara queen!
I gently stroke her thighs, her quim.
I hold myself dripping around the contours

Of her flesh and leave, for her master
will soon be here to wash over me.

Pagan Poet

One syllable
appears
on the page
the word
sun.

The clarity
of the new
day forms
the seed
of a poem.

The soft sway
of language
breezes across
the fertile
earth.

Dusk

The glaring rimless sun reflects
its haloed image through
a sheet of snow cloud.

The flakes of vertigo
pelt the windscreen
and the jagged glitch

Sharpened waves
of the balancing lakes
slash the rim of the sun

bleeding the horizon.

Violets

'We are all in this bloody century together and that alone
should be argument enough to stop the killing.'

—Albert Camus

I have been lodged, a fragment from the weapons of conflict.
That night in April 1973 you dragged me home
    along Etna Drive
through the blatter of bullets; when I woke up
    you were dead.
Every garden fence and hedgerow was a trench
    you got me over
the top, to sleep ever since with the slithers of shell shock.
'It seemed like out of battle I escaped', and from
    the hardback grave
of *Lost Lives* I carry your memory, an etched
    memorial card.
'Clay is the word and clay is the flesh', spoke from
    this mortal coil.
Thirty years ago you got me safely home, a kid
    who pissed his pants.
Lifeless with fear as the bullets ripped through
    the dark streetlights
shot out and death coloured the night, flickering
    ricochets, fireflies
diseased with hatred. The stench of burning could
    be seen all over
Belfast and beyond flakes of black ash fell
    from the night sky
an aurora borealis gone wrong. The dead
    were congregating
their whispers to fall in the night on deaf ears
    like the drip of water
in an attic space, a loose floorboard, a cat rummaging
    in a bin outside
the window, the cry of the banshee unheard in a gunbattle.

But every last innocent one of them has a line
    to add to this poem—
the killers who killed and were killed, the children
    who will always
be children locked within the child within us,
    the mother the father
the sister the brother, the 'RA men, the Brits, the UVs
    and their granny.
I quarry your names out, not to desecrate your grave
    and throw your scent
out for the hounds of Ulster to devour—I excavate
    your names
out of the black mountain to find the source.

for Brian Smyth
and all those in the book Lost Lives

Radio Realism

On the little teak Marconi
in the attic space of 73 Etna Drive
we watched *Match of the Day*.
The bunk beds now separated sounded
like a football supporter's rattle.
Beside the tower of cards on the chest
of drawers between us were two sets
of 11 perfectly placed: Manchester United
and Tottenham Hotspur.

When the black-and-white images faded
into 'God Save the Queen' and the white
dot on the TV disappeared.

The images were replaced by the frantic
crackle of police messages echoing signals
from the street through the dormer window.
Megahertz igniting Molotov cocktails
and the inferno of Farringdon Gardens.
Unlike *The War of the Worlds* the black
screen transmitted a special powers act,
Roger, Charlie, Victor and Bravo
brought the front door down.

Sunday Morning

Belfast 1970, a grey sky hung
mucus of tar, the scent of hatred
and spent shells residue.

A woman loved for a moment
by the enemy, cried like a gull
embedded in an oil slick, somewhere
off the coastline of my heart.

The etched guilt of a one-night stand
tied to the lamppost. Some men
passed, wrenching traitor, slut, cunt,
and greenhorns from their throats.

That slithered on the black tar
of her breasts, seeping into
the feathers of her heart.

Dectera's Gift, 1996

History is a nightmare from which we are trying to wake.

—James Joyce

I dreamt I saw Dectera
in a flowing yellow dress,
flitting like a sickening fear
the jaundiced future suffering,

Cúchulainn like a legend rose
from the hearts of Skatha
the land of shadows,
union of far-off shores,

overcasting black silhouettes
falling from the gable walls,
his sword and shield held
by the stained fist of Ulster.

The unchanged shape of the past
looms like a myth re-written.
The fierce hound of Cullen
guards the gates of Ulster.

The silent barbs of steel scream
from the crevices of Ferdia.
'Tis an ill deed that I fall
by your hand, O Cúchulainn.

You slew your only son, unknown
victim of a punishment attack.
The Gae Bolg tore his innards
like a six-inch nailed hurling stick.

The head of Saultum screamed
from within that very dream.
No surrender. The men of Ulster
are being slain.

The madness of Cúchulainn,
the apparitions of war,
smoke and flames went up
with wild cries and wailings.

I woke and Cúchulainn was dead
but he will never be forgotten.
I saw him just today upon the
home of hatred's walls.

Existentialism
based on 'L'Existenialisme' by Brendan Behan

The soldier!
walks the staggered horizon,
the ruins of red brick,
aftermath of a car bomb.

His paranoia lurks elsewhere.
Graveyard matter, a journey
through hell, around
the next corner, maybe?

Is he, or was he,
ever alive or is death
prematurely set in his gaze?

He reeks of fate's filth.
Too absent to set down
his gun and wash away the grime.

Since sense and pain
can't truly be felt, he walks
with the stance of a man
that wants to kill and be killed.

Poultice

I watched the snowfall,
like dove feathers
on the moonlight.

I heard the cries of relief
from the black ulcerated
peaks of Donard, Sawel,

Trostan, Slieve Gullion
and Mullaghmore
while my wife and children
slept soundly.

A Tricolour in Tatters

On the apex of a house
just across the road,
a tricolour in tatters.

It wasn't its vibrant colours
that caught my eye, but
the grey November sky
flickering through the torn green.

It looks like it's been there
since 1969.

The orange flaps and scrapes
along the harsh roof tiles.
The white is just a long string

hanging on by the skin
of symbolic peace, half-mast
on a bent rusting pole.

MATT KIRKHAM

was born in Luton in 1966. He was educated at Luton Sixth Form College and Cambridge University. He first came to Northern Ireland for a year in 1989 and moved to Belfast in 1995. He currently lives in the Ards peninsula and works as a teacher.

His poetry has appeared in many magazines including the *Honest Ulsterman*, *The Shop*, *The Big Spoon*, *Fortnight*, *The Rialto* and *The Interpreter's House*. A selection of his work appeared in *New Soundings* (Blackstaff Press, 2003)

Firebreaks

To be that pause in conversation,
what's the word? On this mountain road
the steering wheel follows a signature flourish.

If the dictionary fell without a soul,
if she wasn't here to hear it fall,
would it still hold the word 'sound'?

To be, yes, a firebreak. The guys
who planted these—ten paces up the brae,
next spruce sapling, ten paces—they'd know

just where to take ten and the extra pace.
Plant the tree. If they got it right
those irregularities would spell whatever,

their teams', their girlfriends' names
on the mountainsides. Spaced out.
Trees the kids would draw, the mountainside

bearing her name as the mountain is born
from the cloud, storybook tree,
storybook mountains, force pauses

before she asks how a book
sitting on the shelf would just go and jump.
More firebreaks cut past the windows.

Black Bag

Because they know you're sleeping rough,
you who tea-leafed the politicians' voices
and stuffed them into your black bag,
the army are out on the streets tonight,
rounding up the homeless.

Look at them. This squaddie's dreaming
of being the hero, the one who makes the find:
he turns over a heap of cardboard
and there you are, your black bag, Adidas,
white stripes, clutched to your chest—

'Ere, Sarge! Next morning the sun
over the Thames finds you black bag and all,
lying on a mudflat, looking
like you're asleep. But it doesn't happen.
You're always a step ahead.

Ministers learn semaphore.
I hear the news. The ad breaks, they're now mute,
all the posters faded. And then
the radio goes dead. Wondering
just where you're hiding out,

I step outside after some air,
look up. They'd said the night would be clear
but I can't say I see any stars.

The Discovery of Gravity

Call me Isaac Newton Smith,
mathematician, orchard keeper,
silver-wigged antipodean grandmother.
I'm sitting firmly on the ground again,
waiting for these apple trees to grow.
Time doesn't pass here, time grows.

These are the forces, best Adam 'n' Eve it,
that make time grow in this orchard:
gravity, free will, the spin and tip
of a die, the flavour of apples,
red, green, and a lad whistling
as he walks his red setter.

From over our orchard wall
we see the threequarters moon and we hear them:
the puppy thinks of course the kid
is whistling him this song about the appleseed
but then you could put lyrics to the moon on it,
words orbiting the tuneless whistle:

I can't believe you're dead.
But then you were never alive.
I can't believe you don't float on air.
My breath, Copper's breath, the tree's breath,
no the rustling in the trees—
that's just the wind—your floating breath
would be the pillars that tell me of the air.
It's real. You must float on light.
I can't believe you're not about to wink at me,
an eye. You keep on walking forever
because that's how I'll get to you.
My dog Copper can too. An eye,
or the shell of sleep we all crawl back into.

Will you ever look at this!
Einstein's invited Will Blake and his missus
to join him basking naked
in the branches of my heavy apple trees.
I can watch the apples falling
with force proportional to mass,

can see their revolutions,
red side, green side, red side.
'Heads, Ike!' old Albert calls down.
She: 'Time's falling, Granny!'
Are you free, Will?
Freefalling, Mrs. B?

Nix

Phil said it was a great playground goal,
hut to the school wall, him and Nix
playing one-twos round the lot of us
and he crossed it and Nix hit it
just inside the drainpipe. Jesus! A tennis ball.
Did you ever volley a tennis ball
into the gap between keeper and drainpipe
just before it closes? Nix did. Fucking
excellent. And we went to line up
for the fire drill. Nix was wearing shoes
his Mum bought him. Not even trainers. School shoes.

Phil said you'd know when Nix had scored
'cos every other girl in town
would be rat-arsed or catfighting.
And Phil laughed about football on the green,
how all the dogs in the houses round
would start barking when Nix was on target
and we'd go home to find our mums with migraines.
Have to tiptoe round the house.
And when Nix scored in the playground
all the fire alarms in school would go off
and the teachers would shout all afternoon.

Phil asked if that was what he'd been thinking of.
Maybe he'd just heard the ambulance
that didn't make it to the pub in time.
Phil said they said his knife must've gone in
just below the ribcage and up and through his spleen
and that's how come he'd died so quick.
He'd dragged himself slugwise across the carpark
and everyone moved apart for him
this one last time. Such respect.
Phil remembers him repeating
'Great goal, man. Great goal.'

Carlisle 2 a.m.

The armrest renders my lumbar vertebrae in
wide awake cast iron,
honouring my great-great-grandfather, that Victorian
ghost of a flea of a northwestern

railwayman. A dozen plus got off the last train.
Terminating. Families, mum, dad, two girls.
Could this be any station,
here, now, willing us to shrink and curl

till we fit snug in the scroll of an iron oakleaf?
A town this size. How many die each day?
Or maybe they caught the last

train departing, now sway in electric pools of sleep,
through velvet and reflections, subdued, weighed
down by each eyelash.

John Stone

I swear. The dance of his mouth and tongue,
the lad hanged for striking down the doe,
these I've not carved, nor that abbot's rolling lip,
shredding some youth's cassock with his eyes.

Nor three teeth in my grandmother's gob
as she told my father there'd been work for his father,
and would be life's work for him and for his son.
And old John the Stonecarver my father's father died,

and so my granddame threetooth died.
It was not chipped out by my chisel, by my hand.
But they raised us up, sons of men,
our mallets and blades, by hoists and by ladders,

after the abbot's boy grassed. His phizog,
his leer a gargoyle. We swung higher
than grindstone's grate and whine on metal,
and they tell us the pit is split by screams,

but I see again his chisel, his mallet
descending beside his tumble into silence,
freed of his forsaking hand, my father's,
carving that declining and final air between us.

And gathered then their gawking turned to me,
high heavenwards. Now I am John Stone.
By this ale in this hand I will tell what in a stone
finds the face of a devil, what a saint's.

The Migraine Galleries

Behind inch-thick glass, Athenians, dismembered.
Days are a labyrinth, hushed, dark.
As a black mainsail. A bull with a man's face.
The human eats anything, makes art.

Going to slaughter, it's Athenians who trembled.
I was man on the left, bull on the right.
This is the only way to see it, the bull race.
A calf. A cow. Searching for the sky.

Hen Night

She's hot-cross backed, primed for bearing Jesus.
Stand even in her sleep. In the hope she'd collapse
they spiked her morning feed before
it was even in this parish, the needle.

No, she wouldn't fall. Yes, she let the vet
blinker her with his palm. Alleluia.
Down she went. Want to know what she dreamt?
The farmyard chickens out on a hen night—

see them all untangle where the throbbing club bursts,
tottering, emancipating, spirited
as one high-heeled star-footed doped donkey.
Trimmed, manicured and proper, she wakes

to this yolk-golden nail-varnish sunset. Yes,
the sky is falling. Got to get back on her feet
before they're out of the paddock. It's four
she's trying to count to: four hooves called unsteady,

unsteady, unsteady, unsteady.

The Peacock

He used to roost on the rafters,
spring between them with that natural clockwork.

Whilst the concrete floor was setting,
they couldn't leave the front door open.

We're in, with the old cast-iron bed.
The green sofa rests on the dried-out screed.

Along the high dresser
the jugs define their pecking order.

What to put down when he's peeking
through the panes with his all-round vision,

when over the table and computer
has settled a dusting of the future?

The Buzzard

Jesus ascending from a drumlin!
X marks his one-upmanship:

forget treading them down, water and fire.
This miracle still hangs from a cross of air.

If earth sins this day that filters
through the tips of his feathers

he'll know. A sin small as a leveret.
Fieldmouse small. As a shrew. A shrew's heartbeat.

The Curlew

Poor bird, he is obsessed!—Elizabeth Bishop, 'Sandpiper'

Go! she'd yelled. *Get it into your tiny head*
that I won't wait for you to stop digging the garden.
That I've had it with your forking cold spaghetti,
head down, never looking up at me.

Take the ferry to the far side.
If you must come back, walk back,
the whole loughshore mind, every beach, each headland,
all the rockpools and sandbars.

He kicked off his boots, spread his toes.
Grains over grains slipped and swam and dried
and the two worlds shifted. His stare stabbed the beach.
This sand, it stung his feet like nails.

His skin. He must be hypersensitive
to the sealough's inhalations, exhalations.
The sea cursed. His skin flamed, flaked, grew feathers.
The elemental bargain taken.

Never stepped over the same loughshore twice.
They were redundant, her mapmakers.
The sun glinted off the water with a thousand eyes.
He'd fly back, calling *you, look you, look you, look!*

Subsidence Road

What missing sunlight? Winter'd just stayed on,
the last to leave the party and them getting set
to row over just who'd invited him.

Roots ran down their pipes: they didn't know.
But they could quote their credit card statements,
who'd called what number on that itemised bill.

Hesitant showers, neighbourhood kids
fingernail-rattled their attic window.
Unheard. Ah, but they knew all about who
flirted with whom, who slept on last night's sofa.

When you walk the early morning mongrel
on that new waste ground, some tremor
might tickle his paws. You'll remember
their voices, seeping through the muffled earth.

Furnace Avenue

God save our town planners, our arson squad!
God save our engineers and the factory
for the manufacture of asbestos juggernauts!
For they have the holy and perfect technology
which can lift a burning building quite intact
and transport it to Furnace Avenue.

Now all our incendiary problems are contained!
Every petrol-soaked house, every flaming car,
every crazed pyromaniac in town
within the restricted zone of Furnace Avenue!
We can walk the streets, stroll home and sleep in peace!
God save our town planners, our fireproof police!

Unfinished Haiku

Every morning I drive along the shore
of Strangford Lough and sometimes it is clear
which is sky, which is sea, mountain, which sun,

and on other mornings the sea is where
the iron sky should be, there's a dragon
beneath the mountains and the car flies off
the gravity-loosened road, becomes the sun.

Shiko Munakata, woodblock artist,
chronically short-sighted, nose-heavy specs,
face so close to where his chisel became
the absence of wood he'd near breathe it in,

carved Wisdom, a monk trying to outstare
his own crossed and double-jointed fingers,
with a large hole in his cross-eyed head.

Between These Islands

You build bonfires of pianos—
you just dropped by to see if I had
any cigarettes, and whose fault
is that? I spill the kettle. We joke.

Now we've given up smoking—however,
the piano ... my clothes smell of coal,
the house is the devil to heat. Excuses.
Leave it where you found it, if that

was where we put it. The best policy.
There's so much to clarify, putting my case—
petty tasks, the temperature of the phone,
all that remains to point at—the trees

shedding leaves like confetti grown old,
the rope as it cries out against the flagpole,
and the other city, no burning colours,
your hand reaching out to still the clock.

Sestina from a Sketch on a Postcard Left on a Chair

If you can't find that card you use as a bookmark,
the postcard with the goldfish bowl by, who, Matisse,
it's because I scrawled a rough poem on the back
and left it, I'm not sure but on one of the chairs.
Check the ex-café chair, the one we re-birthed, chance
passing-by midwives to the roadside skip we breached
it from. Shoving away the tables, in we reached
and lifted it, up from the tarnished bar stools, marked
out for its new home, new life, for its second chance.
Seat for some Parisian. Fitzgerald. Matisse.
One of those loose-jointed black-coffee-drinker's chairs,
it's now in our office, unofficious, laid back.
But the card's not there.

               You know that pain in the back
when as blank-ceilinged Michaelangelos we reached
to brush the heights, employing that old kitchen chair
as decorator's step-up? Took many's the mark,
honeybee, ocean-blue dollops. Not quite Matisse:
this chair has us down as Jackson Pollocks. That chance
factor to its decoration.

               And there's no chance
it's on the beech stool. Plug-in tools unused: we're back
to bow and pedal lathe. The old style format is
three-legged, ash, then oak-spliced to cope with breaches
induced by the central heating. We could remark
on the seat's adze marks.

               Go look on the wicker chair
that looks over the garden. Still Daddy's chair
to you.

               Neighbour's sander borrowed, you had the chance
to rid that solid kid-sized chair of every mark
of primary-school paint. Still green patched struts call back
to you. Bring the sandpaper. A human hand's reach.

               Scrawled a poem on that card you've lost, that Matisse
postcard—was it just post-Second-World-War Matisse

said something like art should be a comfy armchair?
That's a comment, after all that, on what we're each missing.
          Bereaved Jewish families forego the chance
to sit on chairs. They use the floor. This could be back
to tents in a Sinai sandstorm, with no space to mark
as your own, back to when you saw burdens in chairs.
Storm passed, chance to move on. Found that card by Matisse.
The ground is just the ground. This is the mark we've reached.

In the Year of the Horse

If this prophecy were a thunderstorm,
she'd fall in love with the weatherman.
She'd turn every room in the house upside-down
looking for the ring on her finger.

He wants to carry her on his fingers,
like scissors, carefully, delicately.
Over she trips on the open diary
of a clumsy man. The fridge hums. Vivaldi.

She's painting on the walls again.
Marooned for hours in the library,
he is abandoned to party chat,
Taurus rising, visiting America.

Meet the man who invented history.
The assassin of ancestors. Who carved
the first dictionary, whose jukebox states
collective security, well-rehearsed dances.

'But I've scaled way up here,' our man yelled
from the bookshelf, 'so as not to drown
in all that. Alleluia! Put torches
to the dictionaries, watch us running

to the caves, painting visions of mammoth,
bison on the walls of the caves. Will you
paint a cradle, paint out any logic
in our sleeping or our daydreaming

so one simple dream only recurs:
night, day, night, day, night, day?'

Mary's Consequences

Electricity. Nothing is more vital.
You're fifteen hard worked floors above the headlights
all strung along the embankment's fluid road,
rain-struck, black, and the river is polished steel,
reflecting streetlights. Making you think of what?

Ever played that child's make-up-a-story game?
You write a sentence, fold the paper, and write.
The consequence was. Dot dot dot. Or doodle
a body part, head shoulders arms torso legs,
making this hotchpotch. Knee bone connected to.

We're all made from parts of our dead ancestors.
You're five floors below the lightning conductor
and you were a child once. But I am not made
from making any kind of love. Look. These lights
through the raindrops on the window make themselves

the most beautiful thing seen with your own eyes,
since? First time you set eyes on a Christmas tree
and knew it was dripping silvers, reds, golds
same as these taillights, streetlights, these traffic lights.
Each droplet is made a bauble and a star.

Just how a human heart might warm, it warms you.
Go home. Your family is watching TV.
To the thigh, bone. Wasn't it their parents' flesh,
marrow the gods recycled into the Earth?
I should be your biographer. Make monster

out of you and I'm off this treadmill, these births
and rebirths. Writing how Mary. Met Victor.
On the shores of Lake Geneva. Fold the page.
See how the more I write and fold the paper
the more it makes my voice fade. Dot dot dot dot.

Sleeplessness

The traffic
is not her breathing.

He thinks of someone
sleeping so deeply
a lung swells and shrinks
slower than the moon.

A child, he'd try to sleep
head at the foot end
just to see how it was,

imagine waking
disoriented
but never fall into sleep.

He'd lie on his left,
hear armies march
for nights until he learnt
to sleep counting
his heartbeat.

Now he moves
over to where she slept
after the traffic no longer
kept her awake.

Her side of the bed. He'd never
taken her space so simply.

Imaginary Numbers

White churchmen's collars on the dark necks
of the returning Brent geese
are minus signs before the figures,
a Newfoundland thermometer,
Newfoundland, where the root of the blue
which is the lack of a number of clouds
is a break
        within a short poem
        written on a pebble, dropped
        in our wind-stroked lough.

Drivetime

Urban sections,
conclaves he knows he'll always stay outside of,
days when the wheel won't listen
keep rolling him around and over.

It's by no means
the city's viscera. Or bloodstream. More like
frequency modulation
or one of her hidden nests, but not quite.

Again this morning
some wasp was a minor banshee on the same window
he might open to free
the same wasp every day.

Electricity packages
her traffic and his dancing feet keep moving,
moving, brake clutch
accelerator. Sound is the mechanical

menace around something
loose in his hubcap. Or something rattling,
transparent, on glass,
something they both can listen to.

April Avenue

Out all night ears ring and ring. What a
how-many-drags-have-I-taken-from-this face!
And I want you to tell me how some roads
are like months that get warmer towards closing.

In all day ears ring and ring. Eye-skimming spots
punctuate that novel drowsing in your lap.
Some expression to stump the antibiotics!

A forged letter-i dot, a flea of a cough
sly as winter cutting to autumn,
hops before getting crushed between thumbnails.

Now, like a glass widening towards its base,
after twenty-plus days of thirst, your real news.
You think of your own perfect analogy.
You're spring rain. A good murder mystery.

Jeyes' Fluid

Tuesday mornings since he died
the late-middle-aged woman from forty-four
delitters, prunes the front yard

of the students at fifty-one.
That's all right. But then she blitzes
their concrete with Jeyes' Fluid. Two bottles.

And over the river they know it's Tuesday
when an intrusion of Jeyes' Fluid
forces nostrils apart, infuses

kids' corn beef sandwiches,
late-afternoon lovers' fingertips,
their evening daffodils.

Still, it's better,
says the woman at forty-seven, than him
screaming along the midnight drunken pavement

about who's taking over the neighbourhood.
Out of his senses. Smell, taste. Drink anything.
Every Tuesday afternoon

he bangs his head on his coffin lid,
unable to get the sick
saliva Jeyes' Fluid aftertaste

off his dead tongue, and she's sitting
in her immune front yard, drinking tea
you could stand a spoon in,

tea that tastes better
Tuesday by Tuesday.

Macaw

McCullough. McKeever. McClean.

This halloing echolalia, this stony
acre in the mammalian mind. I'm no
escallonia Donard, no hyacinth macaw.

McCarthy. McCutcheon. McKeown.

What do they want to grow? I'm told hallo
hallo hallo hiya hallo how many
times an hour? I could bark like a puppy.
I could work out how many times a day
they're able to disregard that my blue
wings, my yellow breast already echo
the clematis The President, that forsythia.

Bed of the Year

Another hard spring.
Of pushed-up lumps in the mattress, this is the sum: a
night when you missed the mellow shut-eye you sought. An
unfair deal and I'm the winner,

on the bed's good side. Time to, hush, hush, bring
you coffee, do my push-ups, hum a
seasonal tune. I've caught on
as to why you're bleary eyed. Swap tonight—you'll win a

budding mid-Spring
dream, darling, of incomparable Summer
melting into plump Autumn.
We'll shut out Winter.

You'll spring out of bed to whistle some of
those tunes, untaught. And sing? We'll know when to.

Farm Dog

Is there salt
in my beer, I wondered
as I read how my brother'd returned

to this vineyard,
honest farm dogs, village
sweetheart—he'd sent a photo of them

in the square
by the empty plinth from which
the Father of the Nation's statute

had been toppled.
Whilst snows on those peaks were melting,
where had I been? Drowning in unchallenged

faith that rising
waters were unstoppable?
The flood passed, as always, the valley

trapped its rich silts.
And I've stood still. That drought
in my throat's the knowledge that no salt

is driving
my most natural of thirsts.
Home. Listen. The apple picker is singing

of days and days
before snakes and statues. She has
her reasons and my take mine. This place

is worth ten
thousand, ten million.

The Buddha Visits Carlingford
Chrissie & Mike, 15th May 2003

Mountains, as if I'd never left the hills of Nepal.
I could sit here, or circuit this island,
marvel at dolphins as they surge off Aran-wards.
I'd leave a gallery of footprints in the sand,

lost in the mists below the hills of Donegal—
I'd always return where nothing is twofold
without being one. No sound without the shore,
shoreline without waves. My tracks two rings of gold.

MARIA MCMANUS

was born in Enniskillen, Co. Fermanagh in 1964. Educated at Ulster of University and Queen's University, Belfast. She is a qualified Occupational Therapist and currently works in the health service.

Her poems have been broadcast on Radio Ulster and have been anthologised in two recent publications: *The Lonely Poet's Guide to Belfast* (NBCAI, 2001) and *Alchemy* (Creative Writers' Network, 2001).

A play for young adults, *Nowhere Harder*, was developed and performed as part of Replay Theatre's Script Lab in the Belfast Festival at Queens in 2003.

She lives in Strangford, Co. Down, and is completing an MA in Creative Writing.

Lamb

I never was called upon, in the end,
to assist birthing sheep. A wee deft hand
with the *grá* for midwifery and vision
in the fingertips could guide an unborn
lamb's dive to the world, nose between forelegs.
My mother would not allow it: something
about scrapie, infertility, or
me alone in the company of men
in the small hours.
                    Today, I reached up
into your bunk bed, slid my hand beneath
the quilt, and traced the line of your cheek,
neck and shoulder to waken you for school.
The moment your fingers wrapped round mine
I was blessed with other miracles.

Shadow Boxing

My father's feet
were hairy and hammer-toed.
He danced around
and shadow boxed
and started to skip in the backyard daily,
training for the 'rumble in the jungle'.

Dance with me, Daddy.
Let me stand on your feet.
Hold my hands, when you
do that, and we'll move and shift
and duck and dive together.
Dance with me, Daddy.

First Gear

It's funny the thoughts a wet July day
brings to mind; my father in a yellow
Ford Anglia on Rossnowlagh's long strand,
letting us drive. Perched on a cushion on
his lap; too small to push the pedals down,
steering over the wet, impacted sand,
freed of walkers, sleepers and swimmers by
the rain. Faster, Daddy, faster, faster!

And things are not all that different now—
my daughters with their father driving around
the caravan park at Marble Hill or
on the long road down to the forest park
on wet days in the summertime
in Donegal, thirty years later on.

Reading

We never knew
how you'd be

when you got home.
The dog either stayed

sharing the sofa
or dived for cover

under a table.
If he dived, we dived too—

in our house
you had to learn to read the dog.

Imprint

At the Old Library Dr. Seuss
and *The Cat in the Hat*
were newcomers

the day I missed the bus
home and wet
my knickers

in the Gaol Square
in front of the teenagers
from the Tech.

Helen Corrigan
brought me home
to her mother

who, bless her,
brought me home
to my own mother.

Knees clenched, I sidled
as though I could
cover up the tell-tale cling

of a pink and white nylon
polka-dot frock
and the imprint

of the front page
of *The Impartial Reporter*
I had to sit on

to save the seat of the car.

Flash Cards

There was always a fog in the P1 classroom—
Miss Morris was a chain-smoker.
Her desk nuzzled the cast iron stove
Johnny McCaffrey kept lit everyday.

Flash cards. Dick and Dora.
Nip and Fluff. Siobhan McKinney
knew her colours.
How could you ever know colours?

Later, after Bloody Sunday,
I tried to read the *Daily Mirror*
and work out what was happening
using the pictures as prompts—

bloodstains on the priest's hanky
in the Bogside in a world
that was no longer monochrome, even though
in our house we weren't allowed to talk about it.

The Choreography of Being Pious

When Mother Peter developed full-blown
TB, we all had to have the vaccination
even if we never had music lessons,

even if we never had the knuckles
rapped off us with the long thin edge
of a wooden ruler.

They wouldn't do it now—
they couldn't get away with parading
six year olds past the desiccated

remnants of a parched Sister
of Mercy with her head bound
to keep her mouth shut,

coins on her eyes, cotton
stuffed up her nose.
See-no-evil, speak-no-evil.

We dared not make a sound;
I only pretended to touch her
and wouldn't breathe in.

Helen McCaffrey played piano.
She was holy, reverent—
knew the right moves.

I kept my eyes on her,
mimicking, unsteadily,
the choreography of being pious.

Time Was Away

Down the loney on horseback to the lough.
Cowboys, 'pardners' side by side, ambling
on fat furry ponies with shabby tack
and no hats for safety.

From that height you could see
into the cars passing: see the men
who held each other's penises,
(we didn't even know the word for penis then).

Families in black taxis
snaked through, over the border for the Twelfth,
their luggage and baby buggies
bursting from boots and roofs.

Slow down for horses
as one year welds to the next, season on season.
Bareback swimming in the Arney River—
no cure for 'sweet-itch'.

Butch and Sundance.

Preparation for the Qually

Sister Sarto tickled us hard
and threatened to cut the gizzards out of us
if we didn't keep quiet.

She kept ostrich eggs,
old maps of the world, peacock feathers
and fossils in a glass press.

Forty-five voices droned
'Hail, Glorious St. Patrick',
'Be Thou My Vision',

'Soul of My Saviour'.
The Gestetner churned out
intelligence tests in purple ink.

But alone in the nuns' fusty tea-room
I boked into a clatty bucket
and listened to Gay Byrne.

We Were Kinder to Animals

The traveller children stayed short times in the hut
   in the nuns' yard
where Sister Concepta bred Golden Cocker Spaniel pups.

We kept them to themselves.

Crow Baby

I drove home over the back road,
slowly, round every bend and curve,
every up and down,
and wondered for a split second
about the thick rows of crows
on the wires slung between two telegraph poles
like emphasis on something
underscored then underscored again.

They jeered from their ringside seats
when the sparrowhawk
dropped the crow baby
leaving it
to die
slowly.

Tobermoney

There were blue forget-me-nots on the
path to the front door that couldn't
be opened because the key broke in the lock.

We took a short cut through the woodstore,
me, traipsing over logs in high heels and a worksuit.
Quarry tiles and a bike in the bathroom,

the plate with Parnell on the mantle of the kitchen—
your dead grandmother's house,
her red dressing gown dusty on a coat hanger,

the dresser with the blue and white plates;
wallpaper folding itself off the wall.
Family photographs—ghosts eyed up the newcomer.

Simple blue forget-me-nots
survive the generations. Facing west.

For Anna, aged 11

When your father died
you slept in his fleece
and clung to him
by the smell of him

until the ghosts took that too ...

All Changed, Changed Utterly
Easter 2002

A deaf rent-boy stopped us in a back street
near the Cathedral, blaggin' cigarettes and company.
Tellin' us his life story. Everything,

from the head injury he caught
in a fall from a flat in Lenadoon,
to the dead parents dyin' in a house fire,

and the money he earns
in the brothel of a sex shop to supplement the DLA.
He's the pretty-boy nephew of a drag queen

who wears an inflatable band with a cleavage
for boobs, under a bra top.
He wants to buy a 'camp' yellow Mini

with the money he gets from the claim for his fall,
and a flat of his own,
so his boy can't lock him out.

How he doesn't do drugs.
How his trousers aren't the cleanest.
How he puts his make-up on.

Did we have a nice night?
How we should take care.
How he's only twenty.

Later, we talked about safe sex,
heroin in Belfast,
downsides of the peace process

and we stopped for chips on the way home.

An Emotional Argument Defies Logic

I
Herstory

I cannot push back the tidal wave of filth—
things here are no more satisfying or valid
than a life spent plucking out every hair
from my own body, day in, day out, one by one.

I am all turned in,
bloated under the weight of a four-day binge of chocolate
with nothing better to show for it than the penury
of cleaning the grill pan. Again.

There is nothing the matter in this relationship
that a 'new man', equality and sharing the workload
wouldn't sort out once and for all.
But I am a sucker for the belief

that it is more important for the children
to have a good father, than that
a wife needs a good husband, as though
at heart, they are not really the same thing anyway.

And tomorrow,

to demonstrate how reconstructed and reformed you are,
you will wash up your own cereal bowl and spoon, but
leave everything else to sit and congeal, like a scab
in the crack of a joint, re-opening with every small movement.

II
His-story

Tonight I lay here dreaming—fantasising
about making love to you, but instead
I have ended up with an in-depth analysis

of the significance of an ice bucket, its place in the room
(at the time) in relation to you
and a single offhand comment
that maybe you could get it yourself.

According to you, I had missed the part
where you had secured the table,
garnered an extra chair,
ferried the drinks from the bar
and were only asking for a favour.
Apparently, it wasn't about ice anyway
but being cared for, attended to.

This is way too much of a head-fuck for me.
I don't understand women—never asking
for what they want (attention)
but by metaphor (ice)—
way too subtle for me, love.

III
Her

So, how did we get here? To the point
where squalor perpetuates itself, replicating
like a virus—where the grubs
on the glass in this door between us
are only marked with smudged lips and the imprint
    of your nose
from when you squashed against it,
in your court-jester way, as if blowing kisses.

I see only a dirty window.

It is me—this house. I am it.
It's not as if I haven't told you that before
and even though you say that you believe me—
nothing changes.

The dirty laundry breeds and soon
there will be no option
but for the world to see it.

IV
Him

Hold on a minute. That bloody
tumble-dryer eats holes in my pockets—
or so it seems. Have you seen
the size of this damned bill?
What difference does it make
if things aren't clean and tidy
as long as we're happy, love?

Who cares? It's only you feels bad,
if, as you say, you feel caught
with your drawers down, when
someone comes into the house
and it is, as you say,
in a state—like a pig's ear.

What does it matter as long as
the kids are healthy?
As long as there's a roof
over our heads?
As long as we're happy?
Eh? What does it matter?

V
Them

And any bed becomes a battleground
for a turf war that is a dance; a ritual
somewhere between familiarity,
contempt, satisfaction or boredom. Choices.

There must have been a time

We really loved each other once (yes)

When—you remember—skin on skin (yes)

Heat (yes)

We shared the one breath (yes)

Smells (yes)

Eyes (yes)

Yes (yes)

We didn't know our scripts were different then:
that the back-story was riddled
with gaping holes,
frayed edges, old wounds.

Because it looked like stars, or
like the moon on water. It tasted
like chocolate, smelled of honey-

suckle.

VI
Comparing

Every morning early. Too early.
They made their way up Candahar Street
from the Annadale Flats to the Ormeau Park.

She wore a duffle coat, a too-short
skirt, no tights, matching black eyes,
inch-long grey roots in her hair.

He wore a bomber jacket, a skinny under-
fed frame, piss-stained trousers,
his three-piece of need.

Her pocket bulged with the makings
of a hangover it didn't seem worth
crawling out from under,

and we had the cheek to call them
the happy couple.

VII
A View From the Duffle Coat

They're smug them pair,
look at them! Hand in hand—and particular!

He never lets her gather flowers.
The park is full of daffodils this time of year—

and yet, he won't even let her
take the broken ones the dogs have tossed.

'There's a place for flowers—
and that is in the ground.'

My eyes are only blackened—I'm not blind,
I see enough to know the shine wears off.

When Juliet stops singing from the bandstand
it will end in tears.

De Clarembault's Syndrome—
Or, Even Yeats had a Stalker

Would that I were turned
towards you, alone, away from here,
my back to the vanishing point
beyond the Ha'penny Bridge.
Salmon spawn the Liffey under your brushstrokes.

You tuck me in under this black hat.
My lips are dripping: a red split.
Warm, soft, seductive, rosy.
You have brought me with you
despite yourself.

My fingers mimic rosaries
on these throat-pearls.
I have washed, dusted myself with powder,
replenished rosemary under my pillow,
and chose my best, my only, silk stockings.

I have lit the fire;
plied it with slack.
It is smouldering, plump, red-hot, ready,
under its sober blanket.

The Angelus marks time
over the river and the tenements
from the cathedral.
These bells will never know
what it is to wait.

Grace Notes

The sea batters the bare bitter
clay cliff face, 'til it gives in
and falls away and slides with resignation, asunder.
Its grass fringe flaps on the wind
over the empty space
like a slipped toupee, grappling to balance
on a bald head; mocking.

Redundant car batteries,
burnt out mattresses,
the steel inner drum of a washing machine
and wedges of wood
from decommissioned trawlers
are washed up with broken bottles:
rejected; dissonant.

Sandmartins pock the new clay
with joy and holes for homes.
Lapwings celebrate the beach,
punching out sax notes that arc and drop
to the sharp breathy flutes of swallows.
Each one pivots on its axis:
synchronised; morse code.

Out here, the sea's snare-drum rhythm
is the scaffolding of jazz riffs and arpeggios,
of light and shade and tone,
of waves on stones,
of seaweed grace notes
as though this perfect light is melody:
composing; forever.

I Am the Sea

I am the sea
I lick your boat. I am beneath you
I bleed the lungs of fishermen
I claim them for my own
I fill the space between
I rush in
I show you stars, I am your confessor
I am rage
I am every dead thing
I am not broken
I cannot be cut spliced dried canned
I lick your boat
I toss you
I play the wind: the stones are my giddy children
I bend the moon
I offer you morning
I caress you; drink you
I wear my sparkles for the sun
I flaunt my feather boa for the dance of tempests.
I am music; the bass line. I pulse
I give you seaweed for a skirt
I am the salt of your nakedness. Dance.
I am the voice, your own voice, the voice beyond you. Sing.
I will not be silenced
I will not be splintered
I will not be shattered
I am the sea
I lick your boat
I am the sea

I am.

Lady Day

Her voice wears wounds on the outside,
her voice wears seduction on the inside.

Her voice burns
all ache, all suffering, all bruised.

Her voice is lived in, is peach flesh, is nettle sting,
is bone, is sinew, is grit buried in grazed knees.

Her voice licks me alive, fills me,
and me all spent.

Her voice is a low-slung hammock,
is sin, is purging, is adultery, is breaking every rule.

Her voice is naked.
Her voice is prayer.

The Measure of Me ...

I

I want you. I want you on the inside
dripping off me, shocked, seduced,
caught off guard. Addicted,
unable to leave.

We yield everything, and there
is no place to run to—
nowhere to hide; giving in.

I am light in a dark space,
nuzzle to the smell of salt
of oil, of yearning.
Feed. Breathe.

Measure me in music.

II

And touching you reminds me of my babies,
soft strokes down the bridge of the nose
drew their eyes closed so they couldn't resist sleep.

I have my father's nose—you said
a pyramid you said,
too small for the rest of me—you said.

Pheromones apparently, drew us in, then bound us
with long strands of seaweed
until we drowned together and keep on drowning.

Stay with me.

III

We threw open the windows and the shutters
to listen to the prayers at sunrise,
and gathered at the mosque

at Kerouain, where the moon
hung like a dripping slash in cobalt.

Our daughters traded banter in the markets—
chewed dates and spat the stones into the dust.
The quartzite orb I haggled for
earned me the title 'racist'—a fat white bitch
squabbling over the last dinar.

Shame on me.

IV

Breathe dancing into my feet,
my legs, my hips, my heart, my lips
and I'd settle for my sixteen year old body,
even if it wasn't good enough for me then.
And in return I offer you,

warm heat of the sun for the cold shoulder,
flowers I sent myself with your money
because you forgot, and that twenty quid I found
waving at me, helplessly, soundlessly, from the window
in the door of the tumble-dryer.

Play with me.

V

The ground called out to me 'remember other summers
all chilly wet and goose bumps,
all snot and sand—

remember other days, hold them in your bones,
dig to Australia,
look for America,

and wash away regret and wash off holding back
and face the steps beyond steps—
jump in and hope to drown.'

Kandinsky

Wild chickens on acid
in a 'quality' hotel
are blazing trails
and entrails
past hungry fox cubs
in flirtatious
rabbles of molten
sombreros at a disco
and are cynical enough
to cry *Wolf! Wolf!*
as feathers fly.

Swan Song 1

'Dance, You Monster to My Soft Song!'
Paul Klee, 1916

I
Maestro

Get over here you! Move!
All strings from your shoes
to the third eye, bypassing your telltale nose,

lifting your eyelids to the stars despite yourself,
you balance trays on your skimpy hands
like some dootsy cocktail waitress

in a too-small skirt and too-high heels.

I have lit the candles on top of my piano,
I am all ready for the hop.
Your pout and grimace will not silence me

and a little sweat will not compromise
your own limp lame excuse
for non co-operation and truculence

because of a bit of a bad hair day.

II
Untouchable

You can rein me into a corner for
'the showdown and who's boss around here, anyway?
It's time you had your wings clipped a little
and learned a bit of manners, anyway':
trapped with my back to the piano
I stand, bodily, but untouchable,
as though I have escaped already

six feet away in all directions—
inside my body to a place
where I can see and hear you distantly.
But you cannot break through me:
I am out of reach
beyond you. Somewhere.

III
Migrant

His eyes are a flick knife
His nose is a conspiracy
His teeth are dredgers scavenging the bed
    of a dead city river.
His breath is a pollution of acid
His neck is a vice—winding, winding
His shoulders are gallows
His arms are more razor wire
    at the margins of a concentration camp
    after you think you've escaped already.
His fingers are splinters of chicken bone
    wedged at the back of my throat.
His heart is a mercury tilt switch
His stomach is a cesspit
His skin is nuclear fallout for chromosomes.

And for all that,
it is hard
to stay staying away.

Swan Song 2

I
Decoy

It's the reach of it
this neck of mine.
I will not now wind in.
Muffle? Yes,
in the crook of my wing:
like some wounded
decoy of a bird
alert, ready
vibrant
waiting.

II
Wingless

Still,
I would rather
bear these amputations
show these sores, these scars
I would rather
carry this than hide
like some ringed, tagged
clipped, grounded
eunuch of a bird
that looks the part
but is more broken.

FRANCIS O'HARE

was born in 1970 in Newry, Co. Down.
Educated at Queen's University, Belfast,
he currently works as a teacher in the city.

His work has been published in various
magazines including *Artwords*, *Fortnight*
and *The Black Mountain Review*. He has
also shared a collection with the local poet
Frankie Sewell, *Outside the Walls* (An
Clochan Press, 1997).

Ballad

I was born between
the Croreagh hills
and Brontë's homeland,
Glasker Mills,
blessed in the blood
of Galway gypsies
and Ulster's god—
fearing sons of industry.
The banshee howled
at the edge of my cot
for the times of Kinsale
down to Burntollet.
The sky was solemn
as a funeral mass,
mourning the Somme
and the gallowglass,
the Ancient Hibernians
and the Orange Order
marched out of Narnian
portals each summer,
the Six O'Clock News
in the month of Caesar
reported on curfews
in defence of the empire,
the innocent evenings
of imperial dusk
canticled swansongs
of twilight and musk,
as explosions bloomed
in Derry, Belfast—
strange Baudelairean
fleurs du mal. Ghosts
of young Orpheus
were found on back roads,
eyes full of Hades

haunted the woods
of druidic oaks
and malevolent blackthorn,
casting a hex
on the tragic, Shakespearean
realm of my birth.
And I always knew
of the way of the north,
that the grim retinue
of another ancestor
was flailing the bracken
of darkening Ulster,
grey-mantled in rain.

The Oak

The oak outside my bedroom window,
when I was a child, taught me fear.
At night it would send its cold shadow
across my room, along the floor,

as if the dark were coming for me
with a famine-hunger for my soul.
Its fingers, twisted with age, bony,
groped blindly up the bedroom wall,

searching for me with awful patience.
Until a wind would enter this world
of oak and bedroom and dark silence,
storming my dreams with grey, gnarled

armies of oak and birch and willow
marching through the black middle-earth
of midnight moaning a long, slow
dirge of the nightfall, hollow as death.

That song swallowed me, I fell far
in the void of the moon, down through God
to the root of morning, sinister
as the sunlight creeping across my bed.

The Night of the Hunter

Across the delta
of the thirties
brave John and sweet little Pearl
still run. That dirty

Jezebel, their ma, grows green deep down
in a lily-hole,
tied upright in a Ford Model T. The sun
is backcloth to the devil,

riding the horizon at dawn, noon, dusk.
Does it sleep,
this fear yellow as corn-whiskey?
The moon is ripe.

Now where is that old woman
who herds stray children home?

One for the Kids

A gothic afternoon. Kids made up like Kiss
converge in front of the gloomy city hall.
Royal Avenue's dark as Fritz Lang's *Metropolis*.

Gas masks, mascara, swastikas. Funereal
teenagers mourn Sid and Nancy and Kurt
in World-War regalia mixed with eyeliner by Kohl,

glamorous in grave-chic, sexy with hurt.
It's only a few years since this was Belfast
in *cinéma vérité*. It's now a style of T-shirt

for Candice and Charlotte, halfway to being pissed
on Merrydown cider bought after school
in the local off-licence, their real ages lost

in a snowstorm of face powder. They're just
    so damned cool,
it's hard to believe they're only fifteen
and live in suburbia, near the King's Hall,

although the only time they sing 'God Save the Queen'
is along with the Pistols in the crypts of their rooms
while, downstairs, their parents sink into the gin.

It's getting late now, girls, and all those sad dooms
you believe in when life is a kiss on the lips
from a vampiric older boy, suddenly loom

out of the gathering dark like a teenage apocalypse
or the very last, very last, last ever bus home.

A Postcard from Yeats Country

Leaving behind the nightmare of Belfast
we drove past signposts to THE WEST,
promising islands of the blest.

Mullaghmore. Mountbatten's ghost
stalked the cliffs of the ruined coast,
cursing the sons of the Dannaan host.

In Drumcliffe graveyard we duly cast
a cold eye on the poet laid to rest
in the funereal shadow of Bulben, massed

against the sky in legendary protest.
The winding stair and tower were lost
in an ancient cattle-stealing mist.

Inside the church, old plaques expressed
ascendancy hopes of proud ancest-
ral figures long humbled in dust

while, out in the green eternal east
of the graveyard, elms in tryst
answered with birdsong from heavenly nests.

We added our names to the visitors' list
and dandered down the path, sun-kissed
after a sermon of rain had blessed

the dream of a man who does not exist,
our eyes braving the rainbowed shist
of that mountain swirling in amethyst.

The Westerns

Every Friday night,
to mark the end of the week,
the folks let us stay up late
to watch an old film.
Perched over the canyon of sleep,
excitement would keep us awake
as gunmen, ready to leap
into the flickering realm

of black-and-white London fogs,
Marlowe's dark underworld,
sinister European villages
drowning in grey *Hammer* mist,
but, mainly, anything made
by my da's favourite, John Ford.
Most Friday nights of my childhood
were spent in the Old West.

It all stemmed, it seemed to us,
from his early days on a farm
in the hungry 40s and 50s.
He once forded the Bann river
after a heifer that strayed,
at fourteen, was hired out from home
to come to grips with the load
of a hundredweight knapsack-sprayer.

And now that he worked on the roads,
laying streets in Belfast
through the man-killing decades,
he'd get lost in secondhand books
with heroes like Sudden, or Shane,
men with mysterious pasts
who grew up, left home, rode the plain
in dusty, familiar epics,

or watching those old movies—
The Man Who Shot Liberty Valance,
The Searchers, or *El Dorado*;
all with John Wayne, who stood
tall in the saddle, till the night he
was toppled by cancer; *The Shootist*,
and the stage was set for 'spaghetti'
death-operas, Leone, Eastwood.

Satis

I sit in the ruins of my own expectations:
beer cans and ashtrays, pizzas, three-day-old clothes,
stains on the carpet, faded Muldoons and Mahons,
CDs of Pulp, The Sex Pistols, The Smiths—

All 'fragments shored'. It's twenty to nine
on a Friday night and I'm watching the telly.
Instead of getting a life and hitting the town,
the unappetising choice of Kenny or Kelly

awaits me like death. In the corner, a spider
sits in its web weaving fine nightmare-visions
of my end in some lonely Larkinesque future

in a flat full of porn and half-finished poems,
cobwebbed and mildewed, like the green icing sugar
on the wedding cake. Yes, that one. Miss Havisham's.

Flashback

Another Friday night in Vico's. Yeah Baby!
Our very own time machine, taking us back
to the 'swinging' sixties. *Electric Lady-
Land* pumping out through the sweet smoke

swirling over the candlelit tables,
bringing to mind the embers of Bombay Street,
the summer of '69—the unlucky police constable,
a bit later on, who stopped the first bullet

in our own 'revolution'—the 'Special Powers' Acts,
'the butchers', 'The disappeared', the La Mons,
   the Omaghs,
the whole bloody nightmare of so-called 'civil'

war, raging, like that solo by Hendrix,
the one that sparks off, no, not 'Purple Haze',
the other one, 'Voodoo Chile'. Our own taste of evil.

Popstar

The guy on the cover of Suede's *dog man star*.
That's me now, on a Saturday morning,
lying recovering from the nuclear war
of Friday night while the mutant birds sing

outside my window. The skeletal trees
walk past, peering in, like H.G. Wells' Martians.
Vines of paranoia and green misery
creep up my walls. In my mirror, distortions

of gothic trellis are haunting the glass.
The whole scene has that subterranean tint
you get in Van Gogh's paintings of Paris,

and this is the garret of some poète maudit,
filled with sunshine the colour of absinthe,
dreaming of women, or music, or starlight.

Pictures of You

I've been living so long ... —The Cure

I'm sitting in my room.
It's mid-September.
The child grows in your womb
and I remember
meeting you in autumn
when the avenues caught fire;
the streets of Ilium,
the music of the lyre,
made the city magical.
The war would soon be over.
You had the darkest smile.
You were Cleopatra,
vaporous as that gypsy-
queen of the old romances.
I glimpsed your mystery
at various student dances.
Star-struck at your eyes,
I was Keats' stout explorer
staring in 'wild surmise'
at the vision of October
you conjured outside Queen's
in your dark, rose-woven dress.
Of all my heroines,
you most resembled Tess
in Hardy's 'tragic' novel,
or, at least, Natassia Kinski
in the sad and sorry tale
directed by Polanski.
Though, walking in the rain,
through odysseys of love,
you were Anaïs Nin,
'desperately, divinely alive'
as a Miles Davis solo,
The Zombies' 'Time Of The Season',
as David Bowie's *Low*,

154

Harry Palmer in Berlin,
as Nick Drake's 'Hazy Jane',
Beatrice Dalle in *Betty Blue*,
as 'Madame George' by Van,
as Fitzroy Avenue,
as Dylan's *Blood on the Tracks*,
'Chop Suey' by Edward Hopper,
as Hamlet's Oedipus complex,
a New York skyscraper—
anything that sings
the spirit-body electric,
'the mystery of things',
Lorca's dialectic
of love and death forever.
You carried inside you
the secret of the lover,
the beautiful, the true.
So, now in mid-September,
when the leafy days are mild,
though you're not here,
and you carry another's child,
I picture you in glory,
like Yeats did with Maud Gonne,
like artists throughout history
have done to free their vision,
as you bring yourself
to you own perfection,
true to Naomi Wolf
and the etiquette of Creation.
Now, in you, something moves
miraculous as a rose,
or the fish and loaves
Christ recklessly shared with us.

The Crucified

Because you died with lightning in your eyes
they would not dare to look you in the face,
full with the dark polarity of the skies.
Instead, they turned from that electric place
where you became your own myth and the cries
of sore, abandoned women reached the palace

a thousand leagues away in Caesar's Rome.
While zealots used you as a cause for war,
blood answering blood, doom prophesying doom,
you gazed beyond the crowd and whispered, 'Father,
why hast thou forsaken me?' Then some
smart-ass soldier wet your lips with vinegar,

as if to say your three years were a waste—
the wife, the children, a share in this world's spoils,
affordable even to one of your low caste,
you'd squandered on a madman's dream of oils
and women's hair, and, still, the Beast
held dominion over the tribes of Israel!

But you didn't feel the sting of such a loss.
Your gaze grew, until you saw a heaven
of lepers, beggars, dead men, thieves and pros-
titutes all share your glorious wine,
while the place of skulls around that bloody cross
began to glimpse the awful truth, and darken.

In the Company of Women

Sleek, voracious, they smile like she-wolves
in offices, in coffee shops, in bars.
Dressed to kill, the universe revolves
around their pretty make-up kits and mirrors

and this is natural law. The orphan twins
who founded Rome and centuries of blood
suckled at no beast. It was a woman's
milk which crowned each emperor a god

for a thousand years of dark, until, a child,
born in a stable to a bewildered girl,
meek as a lamb before her Lord, revealed

a light we live by still. This paradox
is mystery, is cosmos, is the eternal
salvation offered by Pandora's Box.

Victim

Suddenly, you're in a different place—
windswept, folkish, saga-dark.
You're a stranger there, without a face,
no pope or king, no Joan of Arc.

Glossed by the annals. You've read in books
how thousands were slain at a tyrant's whim?
Well, despite your Visa card, car, good looks,
you're one of the damned, you're with them

when the horsemen enter the village at dusk
to murder, to pillage, to rape, to burn.
'How did things end up like this?' you ask.
A longsword explains. You live and learn.

Or perhaps you find yourself whipped out of town
with some other poor sinners, dying of plague,
haunted through dark wood, dank fen, the unclean
spirits of history unearthed in a bog.

Or maybe you hear a lunatic claim
her everlasting Satanic allegiance to you
in front of the elders in the town hall of Salem
in the Year of Our Lord, 1692.

It's the same old, same old, whatever the plot.
You're another grim figure in another mass-burial.
You thought you were someone, found out you're not,
and that makes it hard to be human at all.

Muse

In that *fin-de-siecle*
world of The Stone Roses,
baggy trousers and duffels,
e-tabs and Oasis,

you dressed in the style
of a wartime Parisienne,
a Coco Chanel
bringing glamour again

to the occupied streets
of grey Belfast;
in Edwardian boots,
and lips always glossed,

you visited me
in my rundown bedsit
to drink wine and talk poetry,
or my lack of it,

till, like 'Norwegian Wood',
in a candlelit aureole,
you said, 'it's time for bed'
in a lilac camisole,

for all the world
like Jean Simmons' Estella
tempting Pip in the gnarled
Satis House, or, wait, Ursula

in *Women in Love*,
teaching cold-hearted Birkin
how to hurt and to live
'with complete self-abandon'

in the ruins of history.
No wonder then, is it,
that I live with your memory?
Muses don't often visit.

Dream

I dreamt we were flying over Belfast,
like Chagall's lovers, while snow fell like stardust,
painting the streets and avenues white,
washing the city in East-European light

of a century ago. A dream violin
sent its cry like a seagull over the Lagan.
Mist off the river was the sacred incense
The Holy Land offered to our innocence.

Below us, a map of the past unfurled;
McCracken to Mackie's to the postmodern world
of McDonald's, murals, golf courses, ghettoes,
dockside apartments and tight terraced rows.

The revolution was over and still the peasants
prayed to their gods with dreams of deliverance.
Out of our element, we rode through the star-
constellations, like the very last tsar

and tsarina, before the Winter Palace
fell to October's fierce underclass,
silhouetting ourselves on the rouble of the moon,
dancing a waltz across space's ballroom—

we hurtled through blizzards like one of Tchaikovsky's
sleigh-rides in music, a psychotic symphony
thundering out of the dark orchestra
of night, like a hymn to love's *perestroika*.

And then I woke up. You were long gone.
Lost in the snow that still falls on.

What's the Story?
and as I open the blinds in my mind, I'm believing—Suede

Psychosis of screams. A shock of seagulls
electrifies the silence of six a.m.
another Sunday in Belfast signals,
much in the manner of a Sylvia Plath poem,
its presence in cold, inhuman vowels.
This avenue is grey and Lutheran,

built in an era of gaslight and God.
Mist off the sea is slightly Old Testament
but the spirit of Calvin is gone to seed
along with the houses, let out to rent,
stripped of their dignity, lonely, disfigured.
JUDITH HEARNE LIVES, says a gable end.

From a third-floor window, Leonard Cohen
drifts through morning in his famous blue raincoat,
letting us know what it's like to be broken.
It rained last night. The pavements are wet.
Gutters are weeping. Doorsteps are sullen.
A crack in the curtains lets in daylight.

Slowly, the city, like Nerval, comes to
in a sea-bower, dirty and hungovercast.
Flashbacks: Lavery's, The Menagerie, Vico's,
explode dully like a 70s bomb blast.
Police sirens wail like banshees down through
a labyrinth of side streets, going west.

The first incense of autumn fills the air.
Soon, the avenue will become a woman—
alive and mysterious, dressed for a lover
in scarlet and jade. The world of Graham
Greene's hate-letter, *The End of the Affair*,
post-war tristesse, tragic love, London,

will come to life here. Trees and iron railings
will be sombre in sunlight, gorgeous as guilt.
Ends of gardens will harbour deep feelings,
evenings excite, like rough hands on silk.
Reports will come through, a series of killings,
the Opera House stage *Tristan Und Iseult.*

It's ten years now since I lived around here,
three doors down in a Beckettian pad
furnished to the taste of Jean-Paul Sartre:
a work-desk, a chair, a fireplace, a bed,
a view over backyards full of despair—
the perfect address to be misunderstood

and read Penguin Classics into the night:
A Portrait, *Jude*, *Sons and Lovers*, *Dead Souls*,
listening to wind-sonatas outside.
Vaguely inspired by nature and novels,
I made dark confessions of wanting 'to write'
to pretty, young university girls

whose minds moved on babies, semi-detached
from my fumbling with words, awkward bra-straps.
Those wine-dark evenings ended in botched
rakish seductions and mortified slaps.
Kerouac was right when he left town, hitched
across America, free of such guilt-trips.

All I could do was thumb around Ireland
to gigs and festivals during the summer,
share beer-breakfasts with Dylan-freaks, merlined
on mushrooms and magic, music, Zimmer-
man telling us, *this land is your land*,
while ten thousand small flames flickered with karma.

Back in Beal Feirste, I chanced on a queen—
raven-haired, ruby-lipped, emerald-eyed.
Suddenly, the city was Yeatsian!

Walks by the Lagan, through pre-Raphaelite
October twilights were all very *fin-
de-siècle* with her at my side

but awoken, like Oisin, to a changed world;
semtex underground, like the De Dannaan,
Stormont spiralling up out of the cold
ashes of Ulster, Ogladh na h'Eireann
promising peace as the 'dream grain' whirled,
I realised my Niamh was really Maud Gonne.

(As in gone). And with her, a century;
our bloodiest yet, a real horror show;
The Somme, the holocausts, Nagasaki—
darker than anything in Kafka or Poe,
blind and pitiless; of God, honey-bee,
love affair, poem, all sculptures in snow.

Which leaves me stuck in this grimmest of flats,
mired, you could say, in the bleak aftermath
of an era of blood, T.S. Eliot's
The Waste Land haunting me, Sylvia Plath
on Fitzroy Road losing her five queenly wits,
fuelling a frenzy, that's near psychopath,

to remake myself, like Bowie or Blur.
I start by noticing the sun, its warm
(or as warm as it gets here in September)
welcome to the day, lending an arm,
as I stray through my hangover, like Lear
out on the heath in the eye of the storm,

the sulphurous taste of last night in my mouth
from the walk home through cataracts, hurricanoes,
drenching the steeples, not to mention my clothes,
as I cursed the daughters of Lavery's, Vico's—
nearly losing my wits and swearing an oath
to clean up my act and lay off the booze.

That's what it's like, living with history,
as apartments spring up and house prices climb
in this grey and Lutheran, northern city,
like cries from under a pit of quicklime,
and out of morning's glory, a mystery
of starlings appear to tell me it's time

for my waking soul to hit a café—
read papers, drink coffee, smoke a roll-up,
find myself in a black-and-white movie;
film-noir of the 40s, me starring as Philip
Marlowe, enquiring if the owner's au fait
with the sounds on *This is Hardcore* by Pulp.

Film Noir

Hell is where we are—Dr. Faustus
Guns don't kill detectives. Love does—Dead Men Don't
Wear Plaid

We now find ourselves
in an old B-movie.
It's late afternoon.
The camera revolves
around a cheap café.
In the corner, a man

sits, smoking roll-ups,
one off the other,
in romantic grey smoke.
He calls himself Philip
Marlowe, in voiceover,
recalls the classic

scene in his office:
a beautiful dame,
say, Veronica Lake,
offers him a case.
He's taking his time,
figures she's on the make,

but accepts in the end.
He isn't to know
that a few scenes later
her gangster husband
will suddenly show
up out of nowhere.

The story moves on ...
... a joint on the East Side.
Marlowe's dark features
are haloed by neon

drink signs displayed
in the gothic interior.

Jack Daniels, straight.
There's a lot on his mind.
These last few days,
if he's been up one side street,
he's been up a thousand—
not to mention blind alleys.

Heard tell of a falcon,
suspected of murder,
on the run from a bent cop,
mickeyed in Chinatown—
a link to the Governor?
The clues don't add up ...

Cut to the heroine.
Turns out she's in league
with the German Gestapo.
Or perhaps it's her twin?
They've crossed Mr. Big.
This is straight out of Kafka.

A dark wind swirls.
Fade in to Marlowe,
leaving the café.
He's had it with girls,
intrigue, Allen Poe.
He's leaving the movie.

As the credits ascend,
we pan in on our hero,
exploring new mysteries.
An eagle heralds THE END.
We last glimpse Marlowe,
in the dark now, with us.

The Caine Trilogy

I

I used to live
in the very same flat
as Harry Palmer
in *The Ipcress File*,
got up in the morning,
made filter coffee,
put on my three-button,
straightened my tie,
and went out to explore
the dingy streets
of Cold War Belfast,
while John Barry played
an autumnal hymn
in the back of my mind.

II

De dum de dum de dum dum
de dum de dum ...
Ultra hip jazz
and Burt Bacharach.
I splashed on Old Spice
and looked in the mirror.
The ghost of a smile
on my playboy features.
So what if I was getting
slightly too old
for the romantic lead?
What's it all about
if you can't bed the girlfriend
of one of The Beatles?

III

The industrial north.
Exhausted now.
A grimier soundtrack
based on the interplay
of Hammond and trains.
City of blood-feuds,
skies the colour
of a smoker's lungs.
Older now,
but still dressed to kill,
I ventured in search
of some kind of justice.
I wasn't to know
that history had me
in its sights.

Correspondences

I was born between the Croreagh hills
and dark, Satanic, Glasker mills.

*

Our little chapel in Sheeptown
was slowly falling upside down.

*

As bombs went off in a town called Malice,
I was living next door to Alice.

*

Troopships over Camlough. Wow!
Just like a scene from *Apocalypse Now*.

*

Belfast vanishing in the rain;
Paris, Rimbaud. Paul Verlaine.

*

Baudelaire stalked the Latin Quarter.
I did the same for a bourgeois daughter.

*

I'm on the hunt with Thomas De Quincey,
in quest of paradise, or LSD.

*

In a dingy flat on the Cromwell Road,
I'm lying under the floorboards, dead.

*

'Nightingale' by the Dee Felice Trio.
I'm either in Clements or 60s Soho.

*

A guy called Jennifer asks my name.
The Parliament, or maybe *The Crying Game.*

*

Pipe-bombs. Larne. The meaning: Get Out!
This is not a pipe. The artist; Magritte.

*

I'm hot on the trail of Che Guevara,
rumoured to be hiding out over the border.

*

Alex, the boy from *A Clockwork Orange,*
won't return my calls. He thinks I'm strange.

*

The Man With No Name rides into the sunset.
I'm trying to keep up on a flea-ridden jennet.

Aubade

It's just after dawn
on a June morning
and I'm thinking of you.
The birds are singing—
A fresh take on Gershwin's
Rhapsody in Blue.

I imagine the city,
from Dunmurry to St. Dominic's
a starling's sky-acre,
the whole sweep to the docks
opening like a flower,
or a modernist symphony.

And through this mêlee
of oboes and violins,
birds, churches, sea, cranes,
sky dreamt of by Monet,
you travel by early train
in flowering silence.